ISRAEL'S STRUGGLE FOR PEACE

ISRAEL OFFICE OF INFORMATION

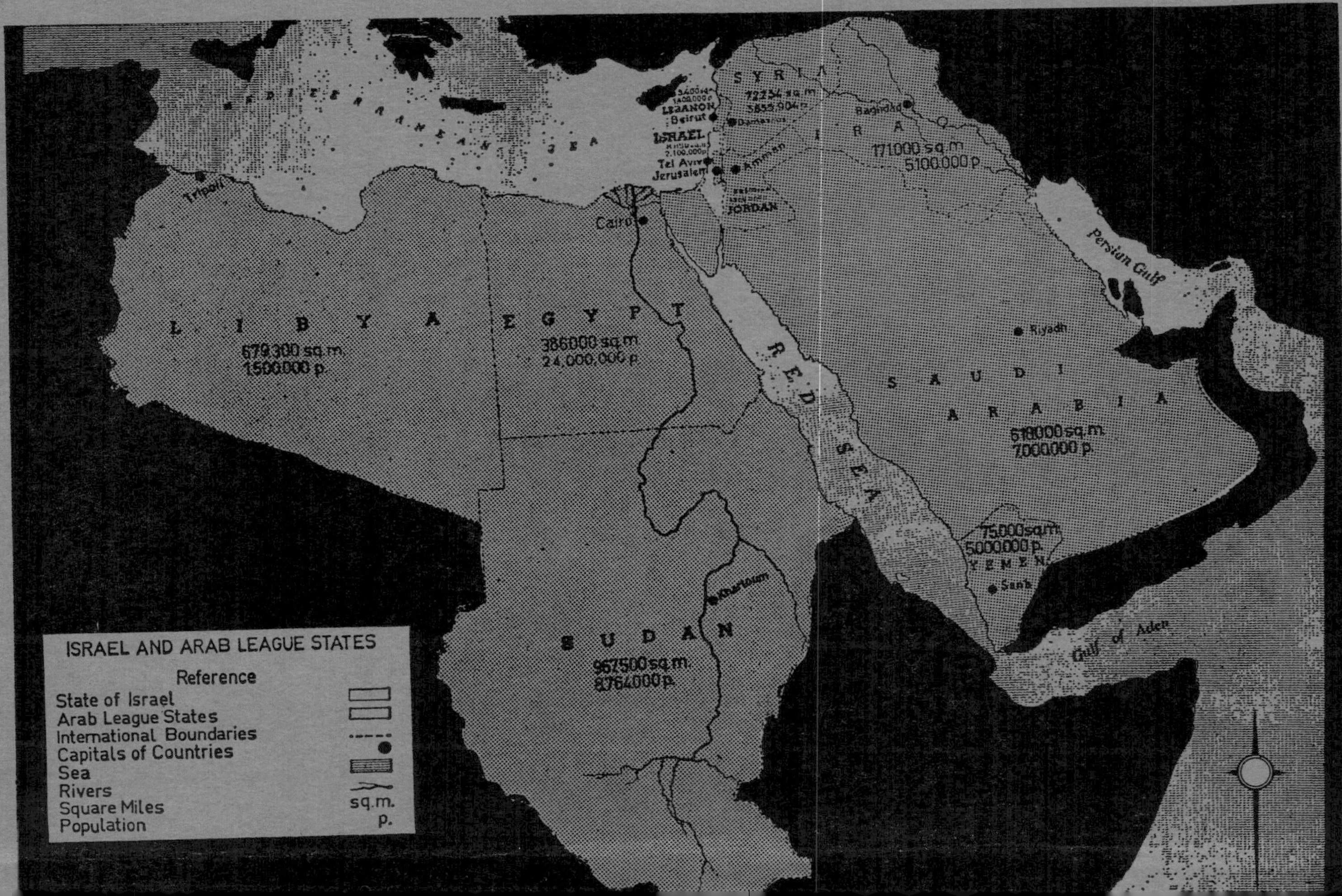
ISRAEL AND ARAB LEAGUE STATES
Reference
State of Israel
Arab League States
International Boundaries
Capitals of Countries
Sea
Rivers
Square Miles sq.m.
Population p.
LIBYA
679,300 sq.m.
1,500,000 p.
Tripoli
EGYPT
386000 sq.m.
24,000,000 p.
Cairo
SUDAN
967500 sq.m.
8764000 p.
Khartoum
ISRAEL
Tel Aviv
Jerusalem
LEBANON
Beirut
SYRIA
72234 sq.m.
Damascus
JORDAN
Amman
IRAQ
171000 sq.m.
5100000 p.
Baghdad
SAUDI ARABIA
618000 sq.m.
7000000 p.
Riyadh
YEMEN
75000 sq.m.
5000000 p.
Sana
RED SEA
MEDITERRANEAN SEA
Persian Gulf
Gulf of Aden

ISRAEL'S STRUGGLE FOR PEACE

ISRAEL'S
STRUGGLE
FOR PEACE

ISRAEL OFFICE OF INFORMATION
New York
1960

Published by Israel Office of Information
11 East 70th Street
New York 21, New York

MANUFACTURED IN THE UNITED STATES OF AMERICA
BY MARSTIN PRESS, INC., NEW YORK

Table of Contents

Appendices

LIST OF MAPS

Preface

The Jewish National Independence Movement

ISRAEL, AS STATE AND AS PEOPLE, is the living embodiment of the struggle, the aims and aspirations of the movement for the restoration of Jewish national autonomy. This movement has existed for nearly twenty centuries, ever since the SECOND JEWISH COMMONWEALTH was destroyed by the legions of Imperial Rome and deportation and slavery became the lot of many of its citizens. During the final quarter of the last century it assumed its modern form, and in 1948 achieved its purpose: Jewish independence and the reconstitution of the ancient Jewish sovereignty. The reborn State has been aptly termed THE THIRD JEWISH COMMONWEALTH.

IN ORIGINS, in ideas and background, the movement much resembled those of other peoples of contemporary Europe and Asia. It is perhaps no coincidence that the renascence of this one old East-West people—the Jews—began midway between the incidence of national liberal movements in mid-nineteenth century Europe and the reawakening of Asia and Africa in the early decade of the twentieth century.

Under identical impulses of self-determination, Jewish nationalism started from the premise that individuals, who recognized a mutual kinship, whether of common ancestry, historical experience, religious and cultural mold, or of other factors of profound cultural or sociological significance, must have a common national basis. Such elements were present in the Jewish case—both internally, because of a uniform cultural and sociological framework built upon a strongly marked and intensive religious and ethnic foundation, and externally, because of a tragic historical experience shared.

From this point of view, as well as from that of the historical aspect of its realization, the Jewish movement is similar to others. The Jews were not the only people whose national independence was wiped out by an alien conqueror, whose very national frontiers had disappeared from the map and who yet rose again, first in a wide national cultural and linguistic renascence, then in a protracted national struggle of liberation, independence and statehood. The major difference was that so many Jews had been physically torn from their native land and the process of revival therefore included a multitudinous return to it.

Against this background one factor stands out: the unbroken link preserved between the dispersed nation and its birthplace. It was a link expressed not only in the historic consciousness of exilic Jewry, in prayer, in folklore, in yearning for the day of homecoming. At no time between the death of the Second Commonwealth and the birth of the Third did Jews in larger or smaller numbers not maintain themselves in some part of the land of Israel, whether in mountain villages such as Peki'in in Galilee, where a flawless line of descent can be traced from the Hebrews of yore to the present-day inhabitants, or in the Holy Cities of Jerusalem and Safad. Even before World War I the Jewish population of Palestine was one sixth of the whole, and in Jerusalem and Tiberias it constituted a majority. During the centuries of dispersion, attempt after attempt was made to bring about the recovery and resettlement of the Promised Land. One has only to recall the Shabtai Zvi movement in the 17th century, the proposals for Jewish resettlement during the Revolutionary Era in France, and the ideas which became popular in western Russia half-way through the 19th century. In short, the Jewish people displayed a single-minded devotion towards their ancestral homeland over almost two millennia, never losing sight of the steadfast aim to return at the earliest possible moment of history.

IN THAT LONG INTERVAL Palestine never became a national home for any other people, or even existed as a geopolitical entity. It was conquered and reconquered no less than fourteen times in thirteen centuries. Each conquest absorbed it as occupied territory ruled from without. And each left its legacy in the form of soldiers and slaves and their descendants, sharing no ethnic or cultural identity, and constrained during the Arab conquest to accept Islam as a creed or be put to the sword.* The 19th century found in the land a veritable hodge-podge of nations, ethnical and linguistic groups and religious beliefs. Except for the Jews, none regarded Palestine as a homeland, as a national political unit worthy of independence and nationhood. To the Turks, it was simply a remote province of the Ottoman Empire; to some Arabs, a small segment which might be annexed to a greater Arab empire, or enhance this or that dynastic dream of expansionism; if such there were to be; for others it might merely have religious and divers associations and sentiments. For the Jews, and for them alone, this was the one and only Homeland, the only conceivable place where they could find liberation and independence, the land towards which their minds and hearts had been uplifted for a score of centuries and where their roots had clung in spite of all adversity. For the Jewish national movement, therefore, the land of Israel was not merely a place where, historically speaking, the Jews

* Universal was the legacy of desolation. Most of the country had sunk back into the oblivion of swamp in the north and eroded soil and sand in the south.

had once dwelt. It was the homeland with which an indestructible bond of national physical, religious and spiritual character had been preserved, and where the Jews had in essence remained—and were now once more in fact—a major element of the population.

THE MOVEMENT WAS NOT content with regarding the return of the Jews from exile as an ideological plank in a political platform—its central activity became focused on immigration and the reclamation of Palestine from the aridity and barrenness to which most of its soil had been condemned by the spoliation and neglect of man and Nature. It had thus to be, from the outset, a creative as well as a progressive nationalism in the political sense of struggle for self-determination. The practical creativity of pioneering, the re-making of the cultural and spiritual life of the Jews, and the political fight for independence and sovereignty, all of these separately and in inter-action determined the forward nature of it. Not the vision of flags, embassies and armies, or the external trappings of independence were its impulsion, but, instead, the main emphasis was on the rescue of a people from physical oppression and even destruction, from dependence upon others and the corroding influences of assimilation, and the redemption from swamp and desert of a land fit for human habitation.

THESE ASPIRATIONS and activities were accepted and supported by the world community, through the League of Nations and its Mandate, and a quarter of a century later through the United Nations. Nor were the Arabs at variance then: as early as the Paris Peace Conference, on March 1, 1919, their representatives wished "the Jews a most hearty welcome home."* All rightly appreciated that, in the millions of square miles of the Middle East, there was ample room

* Letter from Prince Feisal, leader of the Arab delegation at the 1919 Peace Conference in Paris, to Justice Felix Frankfurter, of the United States Supreme Court, March 3, 1919 (Délégation Hedjazienne, Paris).

for Jewish and Arab nationalism to grow in cooperation and harmony in the process of attaining self-determination, of achieving geographical and political sovereignty. For it was at that moment that both embarked upon the marking out of the physical contours of national independence.

THE CLASH WHICH SUBSEQUENTLY occurred was due to the extremist character of the leadership of Arab nationalism. The legitimate aspirations of the Jewish and Arab nations were fundamentally reconcilable. For the Jewish and the Arab people alike there was the common need to develop the economic resources of the area, to bring enlightenment, education, science, medical and social services, individual freedom and national responsibility into a region lagging far behind the civilization of Europe. A golden highway of progress and partnership between the two nationalisms was open. But unhappily an artificial barrier was set up by an Arab leadership that was intent rather upon extending its area of dominion than developing the vast tracts at its disposal and advancing the progress of its peoples.

THUS, WHEN IT CAME, the clash, intrinsically, had little or nothing to do with the nature of Zionism or the method of the Return; it stemmed from internal tensions inside the Arab world that traditionally find an outlet in such conflicts. It is also true that the global quarrel has tended to exacerbate regional differences.

THE PAGES WHICH FOLLOW trace the history of the evolving State of Israel—its establishment, development and current problems. Never has it been more apparent that not only Israel but the Arab States which have emerged in the same period need peace and cooperation with each other. Never has it been more apparent that only one conception of nationalism can make this possible, one based on the demand, not alone for recognition of legitimate rights, but also for respect for the legitimate rights of others. That recognition and respect must ultimately shift the accent of nationalism inwards, towards utilization of the resources, human and natural, of the area encompassed by its sovereignty. Thereby would national conflicts be resolved, for nations will understand that their purposes and languages are verily the same. Until this happens, Israel and the national movement which created and continues to support it will unflinchingly pursue their course of remaking of land and people.

Israel is an integral part of the modern Middle East and of the family of nations. Its attributes of sovereignty in its area of under 8,000 square miles, and with its population of over 2,000,000, are similar to the other twenty States of the United Nations which achieved independence since Israel's establishment. It is for the neighboring Arab States of Egypt, Syria, Lebanon, Jordan, Iraq and Saudi Arabia, holding suzerainty over more than one and a quarter million square miles of territory, with populations exceeding forty million, to adjust themselves to this very modest reality. The comparison is in fact between an Israel, the size of New Jersey or Massachusetts, and the neighboring Arab States with a land area over six times that of Texas. Unhappily, whilst Israel is prepared to abide by its narrow frontiers, and since its establishment has unceasingly sought peace on the basis of their existence, the Arabs are not.

The region of Arab independence, which has taken shape between World War I and the present day, is immeasurably rich in physical power and natural resources. Never since the Golden Age of the Moslem Caliphate has the Arab world commanded such elements of strength and opportunity as those which are now within its grasp. Jewish independence has been established in a mere fragment of the huge Middle Eastern domain, on a land which owed its identity and its renown in history to its connection with the Hebrew tradition. Adjustment to this elementary fact represents no concession by the Arab States, but simply the conviction that expansionist domination, their own or any other, is dead.

CHAPTER I

The Jewish People and the Land of Israel

1. uninterrupted settlements throughout the period; 2. nine hundred years of sovereignty, five hundred of self-government; 3. repeated efforts to return from exile, culminating in Zionist movement (about 1880); 4. resettlement on land and growth towards modern nationhood; and 5. re-establishment of Jewish State (1948).

> "In the Land of Israel the Jewish people came into being. In this land was shaped their spiritual, religious, and national character. Here they lived in sovereign independence. Here they created a culture of national and universal import, and gave to the world the eternal Book of Books."

THESE OPENING WORDS of the State of Israel's Declaration of Independence (May 14, 1948) summarize the 3,000-year-old religious, political, and cultural association of the Jews with their ancestral Homeland.

The Jews are the sole survivors of the ancient inhabitants of Palestine to have maintained an uninterrupted link with the land since the dawn of recorded history.

During this period, they enjoyed long spells of continuous sovereignty alternating with centuries of self-government. At no date in history has the territory of Palestine been without Jewish inhabitants. Cities like Safad and the villages like Peki'in in Galilee have always been centers of Jewish communities.

Contemporary archaeological discoveries confirm the historical authenticity of the Bible narrative. Abraham, the first Hebrew, settled in Palestine about 2,000 B.C.E.[1] The Children of Israel, led first by Moses, then by Joshua, returned to their land after the Exodus from Egypt (about 1,200 B.C.E.). Sovereign Jewish States, governed first by Judges and later by Kings, existed in Palestine until the Babylonian conquest (586 B.C.E.). Then followed a brief interval of exile and a Return (538 B.C.E.) under Ezra and Nehemiah, and thereafter a long phase of self-government under Persian and Greek overlordship until 143 B.C.E. Then the Jewish nation once again achieved sovereign status under the Hasmonean dynasty, through the Maccabean War of Liberation. Even after the Roman conquest and the destruction of the Temple in 70 C.E., Jewish autonomy continued until 137 C.E. when, on the suppression of Bar Kochba's rebellion, major dispersal took place.

The subsequent annals of the Jewish people are a chronicle of continuous devotion to their Homeland, and repeated endeavors to go back. At no time did they renounce their claim to it. Jews in all countries of their dispersion continue to pray daily for the return to Zion.

Palestine remained a Roman, and later a Byzantine, province until the first Arab conquest in 634-7 C.E. The mixed population of Jews, Greeks and Syrians were forcibly converted to Islam and adopted Arabic as their language. But the Arab conquerors never settled in the country, and the indigenous folk switched its facile allegiance from one foreign ruler to another. In thirteen centuries the country changed hands fourteen times.

The Arabs ruled Palestine as foreign conquerors for a period of little more than 400 years, the last of them yielding to the Seleucids in 1071. Apart from two fragmentary centuries of Crusader rule (1099-1291), Palestine was in Turkish hands until the Allies occupied it in 1917 during the First World War. Never, between the end of Jewish sovereignty after the Roman conquest and the re-establishment of the Jewish State in 1948, was it an independent territory, or did its inhabitants, before the period of Jewish resettlement, seek or claim independence for thmselves.

Successive foreign conquests, bringing massacre and famine in their wake, decimated the population catastrophically. In 1881, at the beginning of Jewish resettlement, the total count was barely 300,000, the

[1] GENESIS c.XII, v.1. "Now the Lord had said unto Abram, Get thee out of thy country and from thy kindred, and from thy father's house, unto a land I will show thee."

Jews among them numbering 25,000. The estimate in Roman times had been over two millions. Only half of this 300,000 was settled on the land. The rest consisted of nomadic tribes. From 1881, the population increased rapidly in direct relationship to the increase of Jewish population. Palestine, which was a country of Arab emigration prior to 1922, suddenly became a country of Arab immigration. The principal cause was the Jewish settlements which improved the general condition.

By 1914 the Jewish population had reached 100,000, by 1936 it totalled 400,000, and in 1948 exceeded 650,000. Today it is once more approximately two millions.

Although Jews had in varying numbers remained in the land from the days of the Roman conquest until the birth of modern Zionism, whilst others had periodically through history joined them as individuals or groups, motivated by spiritual and messianic ideas, Zionism as a modern national movement began at the end of the nineteenth century. Its political birth was influenced by the wave of nationalism which reached Eastern Europe at that time. It assumed the form of a political organization, with immigration to the national home, its agricultural settlement and economic development, and with the eventual sovereignty of the country as a Jewish State, as its basic aims. The first Zionist groups, imbued with these ideals, left Eastern Europe in the eighties of the last century to settle on the sandunes and in the swamps and begin laying the foundations for the population, development and sovereignty represented by the emergent State of Israel.

At the outbreak of war in 1914, Palestine was a backward province of the Ottoman Empire. Its importance to European strategy, long apparent, now took on a special urgency for the Allies, and a campaign in Palestine, parallel to that in Mesopotamia (Iraq), was envisaged as a prime means of snapping the Axis at its weakest point—Turkey. The military effort was preceded by political overtures from the British to both Jews and Arabs, looking towards eventual independence of Arab and Jewish States in the Middle East.

Even before, the British Government had looked favorably on Zionist aspirations and had entered into discussions with Jewish leaders with a view to curing the ill of Jewish homelessness. During the war this sympathy was translated into political action, which led to the Balfour Declaration of November 2, 1917. The British Government wished to redress the historic wrong done to the Jewish people and to help the People of the Book to renew the Land of the Bible. All the Allied Governments were parties to the antecedent negotiations, which on the Jewish side were conducted primarily by Dr. Chaim

Weizmann, who later became Israel's first President. The Declaration, addressed to Lord Rothschild, and signed by Foreign Secretary James Balfour, on behalf of the Cabinet, stated:[2]

"Dear Lord Rothschild,

"I have much pleasure in conveying to you on behalf of His Majesty's Government, the following declaration of sympathy with Jewish Zionist aspirations, which has been submitted to and approved by the Cabinet:

'His Majesty's Government views with favor the establishment in Palestine of a national home for the Jewish people and will use their best endeavors to facilitate the achievement of this object, it being clearly understood that nothing shall be done which may prejudice the civil and religious rights of existing non-Jewish communities in Palestine, or the rights and political status enjoyed by Jews in any other country.'

"I should be grateful if you would bring this Declaration to the knowledge of the Zionist Federation.

Yours sincerely,
ARTHUR JAMES BALFOUR"

Desirous of undermining Turkish influence, the British Government had also made overtures to Arab leaders. On October 25, 1915, a letter was addressed to the Sherif of Mecca, (later King Hussein of the Hejaz), by Sir Henry McMahon, British High Commissioner for Egypt, promising independence to the Arabs in an area which expressly excluded Palestine on both sides of the Jordan.[3]

The McMahon Letters

The geography of Arab independence envisaged by McMahon is outlined in the following quotation:

"The Districts of Mersina and Alexandretta and portions lying to the west of the districts of Damascus, Hama, Homs and Aleppo,[4]

[2] Foreign Office, November 2, 1917. *Zionism* (Handbook Prepared under the Direction of the Historical Section of the Foreign Office, No. 162, London, 1920), p. 44.

[3] Great Britain Parliamentary Papers, 1939, Cmd. 5975, Correspondence Between Sir Henry McMahon and the Sharif of Mecca, July 1915-March 1916, and Cmd. 5974, Report of a Committee Set up to Consider Certain Correspondence between Sir Henry McMahon and the Sharif of Mecca in 1915 and 1916.

Royal Institute of International Affairs, *Great Britain and Palestine,* 1915-1939, Oxford University Press, London, 1939, p. 8.

[4] London "Times," July 23, 1937, i.e., Palestine on both sides of the Jordan.

cannot be said to be purely Arab and should be excluded from the proposed limits and boundaries. With the above modifications, and without prejudice to our existing treaties with Arab chiefs, we accept those limits and boundaries, and in regard to those territories in which Great Britain is free to act without detriment to the interest of her ally France, I am empowered in the name of the Government of Great Britain to give the following assurance and make the following reply to your letter. Subject to the above modifications, Great Britain is prepared to recognize and support the independence of the Arabs within the territories included in the limits and boundaries proposed by the Sherif of Mecca."

Sir Henry McMahon's interpretation of this note was later published in a letter in the London "Times" which stated:

"I feel it my duty to state, and I do so definitely and emphatically, that it was not intended by me in giving this pledge to King Hussein to include Palestine in the area in which Arab independence was promised. I also had every reason to believe at the time that the fact that Palestine was not included in my pledge was well understood by King Hussein."[5]

American Support for Zionist Aims

On behalf of the United States Government, President Woodrow Wilson gave his support to the Balfour Declaration. He was not the first American President to express sympathy for the return of the Jewish people to their Homeland. John Adams, second President of the United States, wrote to the pioneer American Zionist, Major Mordecai Manuel Noah, in 1818: "I really wish the Jews again in Judaea, and an Independent Nation."[6] In 1891, the Rev. William E. Blackstone, prominent Protestant clergyman, poignantly stirred by pogroms against the Jews in Czarist Russia, presented a memorial to President Benjamin Harrison and Secretary of State James G. Blaine,

[5] On March 12, 1922, in a letter to the Eastern Department of the Colonial Office, Sir Henry McMahon again emphasized that Palestine was to be excluded from an independent Arabia. (Philip Graves, *Palestine, The Land of Three Faiths,* London, 1923, p. 6.)

Colonel C. E. Vickery, sent from Cairo in 1920 on an official mission to inspect the original Arabic text of the letter received by King Hussein, wrote in the London Times of February 21, 1939: "I read the letter through very slowly . . . It was quite evident that Palestine was not included in the proposals to the King . . . He (the King) stated most emphatically that he did not concern himself at all with Palestine and had no desire to have suzerainty over it for himself or his successors."

[6] Palestine: A Study of Jewish, Arab and British Policies, Yale University Press, New Haven, 1947, p. 241.

urging the convening of an international conference to promote the Jewish claim to Palestine. The petition, signed by outstanding Americans,[7] read:

"Why not give Palestine back to them (the Jews)? According to God's distribution of nations, it is their home—an inalienable possession from which they were expelled by force—under their cultivation it was a remarkably fruitful land, sustaining millions of Israelites, who industriously tilled its hillsides and valleys. They were agriculturists and producers as well as a nation of great commercial importance—the center of civilization and religion. If they could have autonomy in government, the Jews of the world would rally to transport and establish their brethren in their time-honored habitation. For over 17 centuries they have patiently waited for such a privileged opportunity . . . A million exiles, by their suffering, are piteously appealing to our sympathy, justice and humanity. Let us now restore to them the land of which they were so cruelly despoiled."

President Wilson, who supported the Balfour Declaration, gave his unequivocal definition of what he meant by a Jewish National Home in Palestine when he stated on March 2, 1919:

"I am persuaded that the Allied Nations, with the fullest concurrence of our own government and people, are agreed that in Palestine shall be laid the foundations of a Jewish Commonwealth."[8] In the same statement, made to a delegation of the American Jewish Congress at the White House, President Wilson declared: "As for your representations including Palestine, I have before this expressed my personal approval of the 'Declaration' of the British Government regarding the aspirations and historic claims of the Jewish people in regard to Palestine."

By this time support of the Balfour Declaration had become *de facto* policy of the American Government. In 1921, writing of the Turkish dismemberment, W. L. Westermann said:

"Palestine had been set aside as a homeland for the Jews of the world under the mandate of Great Britain . . . This was an open

[7] Among the signatories were: Melville W. Fuller, Chief Justice of the United States, Chauncey M. Depew, Senator from New York, Thomas B. Reed, Speaker of the House of Representatives, Robert R. Hitt, Chairman of the House Committee on Foreign Affairs, Sereno E. Payne, Chairman of the Ways and Means Committee, William McKinley, Representative of Ohio (and later President of the United States), Cardinal Gibbons, Cyrus W. Field, Cyrus H. McCormick, J. Pierpont Morgan, and John D. Rockefeller. (Reuben Fink, ed., *America and Palestine,* American Zionist Emergency Council, New York, 1944, p. 21.)

[8] New York "Times," March 3, 1919.

covenant published to the world and fought for in the open. It received official and public recognition from the French and Italian Governments, President Wilson declared his adherence to it, and many of our State Legislatures passed resolutions urging the national Government to support it."[9]

Under the administration of President Warren G. Harding, the United States Congress, with a Republican majority, adopted a Joint Resolution on June 30, 1922 "favoring the establishment of a National Home for the Jewish people." The Resolution, which was almost a verbatim repetition of the Balfour Declaration, was signed on September 21 by President Harding.[10]

In December of 1945 both Houses of the United States Congress adopted a resolution which called for Palestine to be "opened for free entry of Jews" with "full opportunity for colonization and development."[11]

Promises to Arabs Fulfilled—To Jews Whittled Down

After the Turkish surrender in 1918, a British Military Administration was set up in Palestine. At San Remo, in 1920, the League of Nations agreed to grant a Mandate to Great Britain; a civil government was established on July 1 of that year and on September 29, 1923, the formal ratification of the Mandate took place.

Allied promises to the Arabs bore fruit in the formation of independent States in Egypt, Saudi Arabia, Yemen, Iraq, Jordan, Syria and Lebanon. The promise conveyed to the Jews in the Balfour Declaration and enshrined in the Mandate and originally understood to cover all of historic Palestine—on both sides of the Jordan—was successively whittled down. Four-fifths of the territory assigned to the restoration of the Jewish Homeland was handed over in 1921 to Emir Abdullah of Trans-Jordan. The 29 November 1947 Palestine Partition resolution of the United Nations General Assembly proposed to divide the remaining fifth. At the close of 1947 there were seven independent Arab

[9] W. L. Westermann, "The Armenian Problem and the Disruption of Turkey," in *What Really Happened at Paris,* Edward M. House and Charles Seymour (eds.), Scribners, New York, 1921, p. 176.

[10] President Harding had already made a number of statements favorable to the rehabilitation of Palestine as the homeland of the Jewish people. Similar statements were made subsequently by President Calvin Coolidge, on June 13, 1924; President Herbert Hoover, on September 21, 1928; President Franklin D. Roosevelt, on July 2, 1938. (Reuben Fink, op.cit., p. 88.)

[11] Esco Foundation for Palestine, *Palestine: A Study of Jewish, Arab and British Policies,* 2 Vols., Yale University Press, New Haven, 1947, p. 1195.

States in the Middle East, within an area of 1,342,900 square miles; no such Jewish State had yet been created. Since then Sudan, Libya, Tunisia and Morocco have gained their independence as well, bringing the area of Arab sovereignty to 3,533,107 square miles, with a total population of 71,863,000 divided into eleven separate States.

PALESTINE 1920-1948

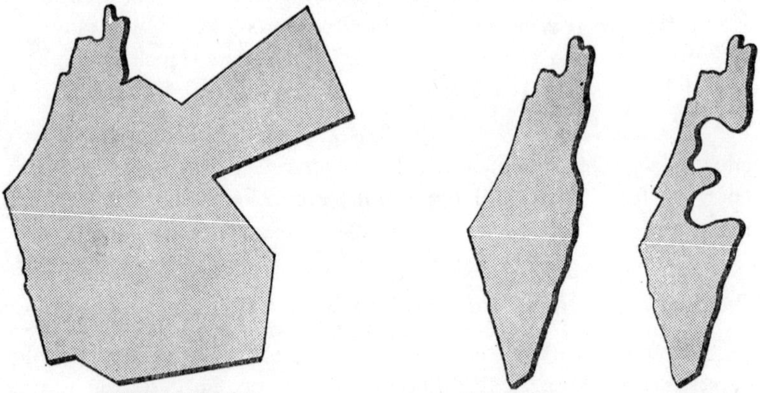

PALESTINE 1920-1922
45,000 Sq. Miles

PALESTINE 1922-1948
10,000 Sq. Miles

ISRAEL 1948-
8,000 Sq. Miles

When the Arab war against Israel ended in 1949, new Israel had an area of 7,993 square miles. Its boundaries had been determined, as they are today, in a series of Armistice Agreements signed in 1949 between Israel and Egypt, Israel and Lebanon, Israel and Jordan, and Israel and Syria. Changes, each Agreement stated in its preamble, could be made only with the *mutual* consent of the signatories.

CHAPTER II

The Sovereignty of Israel

Israel's sovereignty derives from rights surrendered by Turkey under the Lausanne Treaty (1923), conferred on Britain by League of Nations Mandate, and subsequently affirmed to the State of Israel by the United Nations. Israel's Declaration of Independence was sanctioned by rights that stem from universally accepted international legal instruments. Her sovereignty was confirmed by her membership of the United Nations.

BEFORE 1948, Palestine had been a sovereign State only thrice in history, twice as a Jewish State, and once under the Crusaders. At all other times it was part of a larger dominion. The Jewish people was the only claimant on grounds of previous sovereignty. The last sovereign power, Turkey, surrendered its rights under the Lausanne Treaty. They were assumed by the 52 members of the League of Nations which conferred a Mandate on Great Britain, who was herself never sovereign in Palestine, but bound and directed by the terms of the Mandate and the Balfour Declaration incorporated in it. It was implicit in both documents that the Jews were eventually to assume sovereignty. Until the establishment of the State of Israel, Britain held the Mandate in trust for the future sovereign, namely the Jewish people.[1]

At the Paris Peace Conference in 1919, the Arab spokesman, Emir Fiesal (son of King Hussein, Sherif of Mecca, with whom Sir Henry McMahon corresponded), who became the first ruler of

[1] Palestine in the Light of International Law; Ernest Frankenstein, New York, 1947, p. 16.

modern Iraq, announced acceptance of the Balfour Declaration and concluded an agreement with the World Zionist Organization, confirming that "all such measures shall be adopted as will afford the fullest guarantee of carrying into effect the British Government's Balfour Declaration of November 2, 1917."[2] These sentiments were expressed by Emir Feisal in a letter to Prof. Felix Frankfurter, now Justice of the United States Supreme Court: "Our deputation here in Paris is fully acquainted with the proposals submitted by the Zionist Organization to the Peace Conference and we regard them as modest and proper. We will do our best, insofar as we are concerned, to help them through: we will wish the Jews a most hearty welcome home."[3]

This letter followed the agreement signed on January 3, 1919, by Emir Feisal and Dr. Weizmann. Its first article stated:

"The Arab State and Palestine in all their relations and undertakings shall be controlled by the most cordial goodwill and understanding, and to this end Arab and Jewish duly accredited agents shall be established and maintained in the respective territories."[4]

The Mandate was intended to give effect to the Declaration. It was based on the agreement of the Allied Powers that "recognition had been given to the historical connection of the Jewish people with Palestine and to the grounds for reconstituting the national home in that country."[5]

The Mandate also provided safeguards for the "civil and religious rights of all the inhabitants of Palestine, irrespective of race and religion." This meant individual rights and was so confirmed by the Privy Council, the Supreme Court of the British Commonwealth.[6] It is clear that neither the Declaration nor the Mandate which reproduced its terms envisaged separate Arab and Jewish communities, as such, in Palestine. They had in view only one distinct national-political entity in Palestine, the Jewish community. However, for reasons of expediency and to appease subsequent Arab extremism, the Mandatory Administration and a British Government in Whitehall tended increasingly to act as "mediator" or "equalizer" between Arabs and Jews.

[2] Agreement Between Emir Feisal and Dr. Chaim Weizmann, January 3, 1919. Jewish Agency for Palestine, *Memorandum to the Palestine Royal Commission,* London, 1936, p. 296. (See Appendix 5.)

[3] Letter from Emir Feisal to Justice Frankfurter. (See Appendix 6.)

[4] Jewish Agency for Palestine, *Memorandum to the Palestine Royal Commission,* p. 296.

[5] Preamble of the League of Nations Mandate for Palestine.

[6] District Governor, Jerusalem-Jaffa v Suleiman, 1926 Appeals, p. 328.

This was contrary to the spirit of the League of Nations Mandate, which did not demand of Britain a dual, balanced obligation. It spoke of a Jewish National Home, the Jewish people, the Jewish population, the Jewish Agency, Jewish immigration. It did not speak of the Arabs at all, except to lay down that English, Arabic and Hebrew were to be the official languages. The Mandate, in fact, gave the Jews a special position. Palestine was recognized as the locale of their National Home.

At various times it has been sought to interpret the McMahon correspondnece as a pledge of Arab independence in Palestine. Not only did Sir Henry McMahon make it publicly clear that it was not his intention to give any such pledge.[7] Emir Feisal himself, son of King Hussein and the first king of Iraq, had previously declared, according to Winston Churchill, that he was "prepared to accept the statement that it had been the intention of His Majesty's Government to exclude Palestine from any promise to the Arabs."[8]

Nor was there any ambiguity about the term "National Home". Lord Balfour, signatory of the Declaration that bears his name, and David Lloyd George, then British Prime Minister, defined the exact meaning of the term:

> "It was contemplated that . . . if the Jews had meanwhile responded to the opportunity afforded them by the idea of a National Home and had become a definite majority of the inhabitants, then Palestine would thus become a Jewish Commonwealth."[9]

It was the intention of the parties to the Declaration that the National Home should eventually become a Jewish State. In Lord Balfour's words:

> "It did not necessarily involve the early establishment of an independent Jewish State, which was a matter of gradual development."[10]

President Wilson declared:

> "I am persuaded that the Allied Nations, with the fullest concurrence of our Government and our people, are agreed that in Palestine shall be laid the foundations of a Jewish Commonwealth."[11]

[7] London "Times," July 23, 1937. (See above.)

[8] Parliamentary Debates, House of Commons, July 11, 1922.

[9] David Lloyd George, The Truth About the Peace Treaties, 2 vols. London 1938, II, p. 1139.

[10] Ibid., p. 1137.

[11] New York Times, March 3, 1919.

Field Marshal Jan Christian Smuts, member of the British War Cabinet, prophesied:

> "In generations to come you will see a great new state rising there once more."[12]

The Palestine Royal Commission[13] Report[14] gave further emphasis to this intention. It declared: "It would depend mainly on the zeal and enterprise of the Jews whether the Home would grow big enough to become a State."

It is clear, then, that "National Home" meant the establishment in Palestine of conditions which would make possible its evolution into a fully fledged Jewish State.

Subsequent infringements of the spirit and letter of the Declaration and the Mandate, such as restrictions on Jewish immigration and land acquisition, were thus violations of international law. Originally, indeed, the Jewish National Home was to have had the opportunity of free development within the whole area of historic Palestine on both sides of the Jordan.

12 Zionist Bulletin, Johannesburg, South Africa, Dec. 10, 1919.

13 The Palestine Royal Commission was appointed by the British Government to determine the cause of the 1936 Arab riots and to ascertain the best ways of carrying out the Mandate. It was headed by Lord Peel and is thus often referred to as the Peel Commission.

14 Palestine Royal Commission Report, Cmd. 5479, London 1937, Chap. 11, pp. 24-25.

CHAPTER III

The Jewish Natianal Home Before The League of Natians Mandate

Mass Jewish resettlement in Palestine antedates the Balfour Declaration by 40 years. From 1881 to the outbreak of World War I in 1914, the Jewish population quadrupled to 100,000. The Jews of Palestine and of the free world rallied to the Allied ranks and raised military forces which played an important part in the liberation of Palestine from Ottoman rule.

THE BEGINNINGS of mass Jewish resettlement in Palestine preceded the Balfour Declaration by nearly 40 years. The first wave of settlers from Czarist Russia arrived in 1881, linking up with fellow-Jews who had been guardians of uninterrupted Jewish settlement in the country for nearly two thousand years. Palestine was a country abandoned to the desert. The mountains had long since been deforested, the ancient terraces destroyed and the soil eroded. Much was infested by malaria because swamps were undrained. The forbidding aspect of the countryside in 1867 was vividly described by Mark Twain:[1]

> "There is not a solitary village throughout its whole extent—not for thirty miles in either direction (near Merom). There are two or three small clusters of Bedouin tents, but not a single permanent habitation. One may ride ten miles, hereabouts, and not see

[1] Mark Twain, *The Innocents Abroad,* 2 Vols., Harper & Brothers, New York, II, pp. 213-14, 217.

ten human beings. To this region, one of the prophecies is applied: 'I will bring the land into desolation; and your enemies which dwell therein shall be astonished at it . . .' No man can stand here by deserted Ain Mellahah and say the prophecy has not been fulfilled."

"Gray lizards, those heirs of ruin, of sepulchers and desolation, glided in and out among the rocks or lay still and sunned themselves. Where prosperity has reigned and fallen; where glory has flamed and gone out; where beauty has dwelt, and passed away; where gladness was, and sorrow is; where the pomp of life has been, and silence and death brood in its high places, there this reptile makes his home, and mocks at human vanity."

By the spring of 1883 six new Jewish agricultural settlements, with a population of 200 families, had been established. At the close of the century the total had grown to 22 settlements covering 75,000 acres, with a population of 5,000.

Sustained Jewish immigration spurred on economic development and by 1914 export and import were developing in expanding volume. The first years of the 20th century saw as well a widening interest in Palestine on the part of Jews outside Russia. The Zionist movement had made a deep impact on every Jewish community in the world. Societies were founded in New York, Chicago and St. Louis to organize settlements, and prominent Americans emerged to give leadership to the movement.

On the eve of the First World War, the Jewish population of Palestine had reached 100,000, of whom half lived in Jerusalem, forming a decisive majority of its population. There were also considerable communities in the holy cities of Safad, Tiberias and Hebron. About 12,000 Jews had settled on the land, living in 50 agricultural villages, with a total area of 100,000 acres.

The outbreak of war temporarily halted the progress of the National Home. Many Jewish settlers, of Allied citizenship, were forced to leave the country when Turkey joined the Axis. Others were compelled to adopt Turkish citizenship and serve with the Turkish armed forces. But Jewish sympathies were wholly on the Allied side. Jewish volunteers served in the Zion Mule Corps with the British forces in the Gallipoli campaign.

After the publication of the Balfour Declaration in 1917, a body of Jewish volunteers for military service in Palestine was recruited in Britain into the British Army as the 38th Battalion, Royal Fusiliers, under the command of Lt. Colonel J. M. Patterson, former commander of the Zion Mule Corps. It sailed for Palestine in February 1918 and was followed a few months later by the 39th and 40th Battalions. With American entry into the war, the movement to form Jewish battalions spread to the United States. In all, 2,700 American Jewish volunteers were enrolled in the three battalions. In Palestine itself, an entire battalion, raised and supplied there, took part in General Allenby's offensive of September 1918, which routed the Turks and liberated Jerusalem.

CHAPTER IV

The Jewish National Home Under The British Mandate

Between 1919 and 1947 the Jewish population of Palestine rose from 100,000 to 650,000 as a result, mainly, of regulated immigration. There was massive expansion of Jewish agricultural settlement and industry. At the same time the Arab population was nearly trebled, mainly by uncontrolled immigration from neighboring Arab States, attracted by better conditions of living due to Jewish settlement. Jewish immigration and development were severely restricted by the Mandatory.

DURING THE FIRST WORLD WAR the Jewish population of Palestine declined from 100,000 to half that number. The end of hostilities was followed by a rapid increase to the previous level. Under the stimulus of the Balfour Declaration and the Mandate, there came an influx of newcomers from Eastern and Central Europe. Many were young pioneers (halutzim), determined to abandon urban life in the Diaspora and to become Jewish farmers in their own Homeland. They pursued the task, begun by their forerunners, of clearing malarial swamplands that were acquired from absentee landlords, often for exorbitant sums, and converting them into fertile farmsteads.

With this momentum, the Jewish population rose to 162,000 by 1929. *Pari passu,* the Arab population went up by almost 50% to 800,000 thanks to the dramatic improvement in the health and living standards produced by Jewish immigration and settlement and the unrestricted influx of Arabs from the Arabian Peninsula, Syria and

Jordan as a result of these improvements. Before the Mandate, the Arabs had emigrated from Palestine; after 1922, Palestine was the destination of Arab emigrants from Syria and Trans-Jordan.

It became manifest during the early years of the Mandate that large-scale Jewish development of Palestine was entirely feasible. Economic studies indicated that the country could absorb many times its existing population and simultaneously improve its standards. By 1947 the Jewish population was in excess of 650,000. This growth was accompanied by economic improvement for the now much enlarged Arab population. Agricultural potential had been greatly expanded by irrigation, drainage and modern techniques. There had been corresponding industrial advancement, which had enormously bettered the country's capacity to absorb continued immigration in volume.

By 1939 export of citrus fruit from Jewish groves amounted to 10,000,000 cases a year. This was the major crop, but there was also a rapid expansion of mixed farming, including dairy and poultry farming, fruit orchards and sheep breeding, all, in the main, developed by cooperative settlements (kibbutzim) on land made available by the Jewish National Fund. That and the Foundation Fund (Keren Hayesod) are institutions, going back to the earliest years of Zionism, which were established to purchase land and provide capital for the development of the National Home.

Large afforestation schemes were carried out, particularly in the hilly region, to arrest erosion and stimulate rainfall.

Industry kept pace with agricultural development. In 1927 the Palestine Electric Corporation harnessed the Jordan and Yarmuk Rivers to furnish power for industry.[1] In 1930, the Palestine Potash Company began operations to extract the mineral wealth of the Dead Sea.

The following table shows the growth of Jewish industry in this period:[2]

	1922	1929	1933	1937	1942
No. of enterprises	1,850	2,475	3,388	5,606	6,600
No. employed	4,434	10,968	19,595	30,040	56,000

The products included textile and leather goods, glass, cement, machinery, chemicals, foodstuffs, polished diamonds, pharmaceuticals and cosmetics.

[1] The electric power station at Naharayim, in the Jordan Valley. It was destroyed by the Arab Legion in 1948.

[2] Abraham Revusky, *Jews in Palestine,* New York, 1945, p. 71.

The spectacular rural expansion took place almost entirely on land purchased from private owners at high prices. This land, purchased with money collected as voluntary donations from World Jewry, became the property of the Jewish people. The land thus purchased was mostly inundated swamp or arid areas owned by absentee landlords who used the opportunity to inflate its market price.[3] Money thus gained often permitted the landlord to exploit his remaining lands scientifically and produce yields far in excess of those obtained originally. Tenants on land purchased by the Jewish National Fund were compensated with other land or with cash, as indicated by the findings of the Palestine Royal Commission of 1937.

The Mandatory failed to implement Article 6 of its Mandate prescribing "close settlement by Jews on the land, including State land and wastelands not required for public purposes." After 1939, new regulations, outlined in the White Paper, virtually ended further acquisition of land by Jews.

These regulations divided the land of Palestine into three zones. The first included all municipal areas, the Haifa industrial area and the maritime plain between Tanturah and the southern boundary of Ramleh subdistrict. Here there were to be no restrictions on land acquisition by Jews. The second zone (Zone A) included the whole of the hill country together with certain areas in Gaza and Beersheba subdistricts. Here there was an absolute prohibition of any transfer of land to Jews. The third area (Zone B) included the plains of Esdraelon and Jezreel, Eastern Galilee, the maritime plain between Haifa and Tanturah, and between the southern boundary of Ramleh subdistrict and Beer Tuvia, and the southern portion of Beersheba subdistrict. Here transfers to Jews could take place only with the consent of the High Commissioner, which in no instance was ever given. The White Paper of 1939, thus, in effect, sought to freeze the Jewish National Home, in land area and population, as a Jewish ghetto within the context of a Palestine Arab State. No greater travesty of the Mandate could have been envisaged.

JEWISH SETTLEMENT BENEFITS ARABS

Jewish settlement in Palestine is unique in its realm. It raised the standard of living of the Arabs and eschewed exploitation of local labor. The Arab population grew by leaps and bounds, from 650,000 to over a million between 1929 and 1940. Trans-Jordan, sundered

[3] Palestine Royal Commission Report, p. 91.

from Palestine in 1921, could show nothing like it. On the contrary, there was a general drift from Arab countries to Palestine. Infant mortality among the Moslem population in Palestine declined from 196 per thousand in 1922 to 140 in 1939, as a result of improvement in health conditions, an improvement to which Jewish example and investment contributed not a little. This was an important additional factor in the increase of the Arab population.

The Royal Commission of 1937 ascribed Arab progress to Jewish efforts.[4] The prosperity of Arab villages was in direct ratio to the nearness to Jewish settlements. Arabs had benefited from Jewish capital. They had learned from Jewish farmers how to use machines. Arab industry had expanded, wages were higher, hours of labor less. Illiteracy declined.

The Mandatory enacted no laws to control or curb Arab immigration. Between 1922 and 1939, many more Arabs entered Palestine than did Jews.

Some idea of the significance of Jewish settlement as an incentive to Arab entry and well-being may be gained from the following figures: from 1922 to 1939, in Haifa (216%), Jaffa (134%), and Jerusalem (97%), the Arab citizenry multiplied remarkably by consequence of Jewish development of those centers, while towns unaffected by that stimulus grew more slowly, for example, Jenin (40%), Hebron (40%), Bethlehem (32%).[5]

The sale of land to Jewish settlers was a further source of Arab prosperity.[6] By selling out undeveloped holdings, Arab landowners got the money to improve the balance of their estates, and could free themselves from indebtedness to Arab moneylenders.

"In 1933, £854,796 was paid for the purchase of Arab land, mostly from owners of large estates, £1,647,836 in 1934 and £1,699,-448 in 1935. Partly, no doubt, as the result of land sales the effendi class has been able to make substantial investments of capital. Some of this has gone towards increased production, especially of fruit, from the land they have retained. At least six times more Arab-owned land is now planted with citrus than in 1920 . . . Some of the capital has been directed to building houses for lease or sale or to industrial enterprise . . . The number of Arab industrial undertakings, which was about 1,200 before the war, had risen to about 2,200 . . . In the light of these facts we have no doubt that many Arab landowners have

[4] Ibid., pp. 90-94.
[5] Ibid., p. 93.
[6] Ibid., p. 91.

benefited financially from Jewish immigration. They have sold a large amount of land to Jews at a price far higher than its pre-war value. A member of the Arab Higher Committee admitted to us that 'nowhere in the world were such uneconomic land prices paid as by Jews in Palestine'." (Palestine Royal Commission Report, 1937, Chapter V, p. 91.) Not only did the effendis (landlords) benefit from Jewish land purchase and settlement, the fellaheen, or peasants, benefited as well. Job opportunities opened in the towns, the expansion of citrus cultivation increased the demand for their labor, and wages rose, from 80 to 120 mils a day in 1931 to 150 mils in 1935 and for tree planting and nursery work to even 200 mils in that year.[7]

The Report itself, on page 94, reaches the conclusion: "The Arabs shared to a considerable degree in the material benefits which Jewish immigration has brought to Palestine. The obligation of the Mandate in this respect has been observed."

In 1948, after the State of Israel had been established in only part of the area of the original Mandate, 8.6% of the land was owned by Jews, and 3.3% by Israeli Arabs; 16.9% had been abandoned by Arab owners. Over 70% had been vested in the Mandatory[8] and, accordingly, reverted to the State of Israel as its legal heir.

The greater part of this seventy percent was the Negev area, some 3,144,250 acres, which itself consisted of close to fifty percent of the total area of Palestine's 6,580,000 acres. These lands, known as Crown Lands, consisting of arid and uninhabited territory, had been inherited originally by the Palestine Mandatory Government from Turkey and, when Israel was established in 1948, were therefore passed from the Government of Palestine to the Government of Israel. Agricultural and industrial development of this territory was initiated on a large scale in 1948, small scale activities in the area having been started by Jewish settlers during the Mandatory period.

For the 16.9 percent of Israel's territory, which had been abandoned by Arab owners, the Government of Israel has consistently offered to pay compensation and to facilitate this established a Government Departemnt of the Custodian of Abandoned Property. On the other hand, with the signing of the Armistice Agreements in 1949, the borders of Israel mutually agreed left Jewish land, such as that cultivated by the Etzion bloc of villages south of Jerusalem, and Jewish property in the Jewish quarter of the Old City of Jerusalem, in Arab hands.

[7] Ibid., p. 92.
[8] Government of Palestine, *Survey of Palestine,* 1946, Government Printer, p. 257.

✓

CHAPTER V

The Arabs and the Jewish National Home

Initial Arab sympathy for the Jewish National Home was converted into hostility by extremist demagogues, led by the Mufti of Jerusalem, who organized attacks against Jewish communities in 1920, 1921, 1929 and during 1936-9. The Mandatory adopted a policy of appeasing Arab extremism which compelled the Jews to organize their own Defense Force—Haganah. The Chamberlain Government in May 1939 abandoned the principles of the Balfour Declaration and the Mandate by restricting further Jewish immigration and acquisition of land. Despite British concessions, the Arab extremists actively assisted the Nazi-Fascist Powers during World War II.

FOLLOWING THE EXAMPLE of Emir Feisal (see page 9), the Arabs were at first friendly to the idea of the Jewish National Home, from which so many benefits would accrue to them. Later, intransigence made headway among them under the provocation of political ambition and religious fanaticism.[1]

[1] This intransigence was by no means universal. This is reflected by a letter to the United Nations Special Committee on Palestine (UNSCOP) from Mgr. Ignatius Moubarakis, Archbishop of Beirut, dated 5 August 1947. In this letter Mgr. Moubarakis stated that "Lebanon had been dragged willy nilly within its neighbors' orbit, but that its current leaders represented no one but themselves. As for Palestine, its inhabitants had been forcibly converted to Islam, although Palestine was the cradle of the Jews and the early Christians, neither of them of Arab origin. The Holy Places and all the monuments of the two religions bore witness to the fact that

The first anti-Jewish riots broke out in Jerusalem and neighboring villages in April 1920. They were followed by an attack in Jaffa in May 1921. Arab extremism, trading on the ignorance of backward elements to foster anti-Jewish feeling which from time to time erupted in open violence, found its most prominent spokesman in Haj Amin al-Husseini, Mufti of Jerusalem. He did not confine himself to administering religious affairs. He made his office a platform for anti-Jewish intrigue and agitation. It was he who first inflamed the mob during the Jerusalem riots of 1920, fled to Trans-Jordan, and was sentenced to fifteen years imprisonment *in absentia.* Amnestied by the High Commissioner, he returned to Jerusalem and was appointed Mufti,[2] after other nominees had been induced to withdraw. The following year he was elected President of the Supreme Moslem Council, thereby acquiring control over charities with an annual income exceeding $500,000 and over the religious courts, as well as authority to appoint preachers in all mosques. He consolidated his power over the Arab community and systematically began to sabotage the Mandate.

The agitation whipped up by Arab extremists increased in ferocity until on August 23, 1929, the inevitable outburst occurred: Arab mobs attacked the Jewish quarters of Jerusalem, and the Arabs of Hebron massacred the small, defenseless Jewish community there. The disorders spread to many parts of the country and were fanned by infiltrating Bedouin. There was no British military force that could meet the situation, and the police, drawn largely from the Arab community,

Palestine was not Arab, and should not be included among the Arab countries, any more than Lebanon. Lebanon had always been the refuge of persecuted Christians. Lebanon and Palestine should continue to be the permanent homes of minorities."

In his letter to the Special Committee, read by Mr. Garcia Granados, its Guatemalan member, Mgr. Moubarakis referred to Jewish achievements and declared that "there were as many men of culture and intellect among the Jews and Lebanese as in the rest of the Near Eastern countries put together. An ignorant majority should not be allowed to impose its will. A million progressive human beings should not be the plaything of a few leaders supported by millions of human beings of less advanced ideas. There was a certain order in the world which helped to maintain the necessary equilibrium. If the United Nations wished to save that order, it must consolidate it. A Christian home in Lebanon, a Jewish home in Palestine—the two countries geographically and economically linked would form the necessary bridge between the East and the West, and would maintain in the Near East that peace which existing rivalries rendered so precarious." The Mgr. stated that "the so-called legitimate representatives of Lebanon had only repeated what they had been told to say by their lords and masters in the neighboring Arab countries. True Lebanese opinion had been stifled by the group which had faked the elections of 25 May. The Lebanese demanded liberty for the Jews of Palestine, just as they hoped for liberty and independence themselves."

United Nations Official Records, General Assembly, Second Session, Summary Records of Meetings, 25 September - 25 November 1947, pp. 57-58.

[2] Mufti—religious head of the Moslem Community in part of Palestine.

were unreliable. One hundred and thirty Jews were killed and 198 wounded. But the Jews defended themselves and, in the process, Haganah, the Jewish Defense Force, in secret existence since the 1920 disturbances, came to maturity.

After a brief lull, Jewish efforts at settlement proceeded at swifter tempo. From 1920 to 1932 the average annual Jewish immigration had been 10,000. After the advent of Hitler to power in 1933, there was a sharp rise. That year 30,927 entered; in 1934, 42,359; in 1935 nearly 62,000. Besides, about 5,000 victims of Nazi persecution made their way in "illegally" each year, because the Mandatory withheld certificates.

In 1936 Arab terrorism became a guerrilla war, waged against the Government, the Jewish community, and a large part of the Arab population itself. Its concomitants were arson, deforestation, and destruction of wells and pipelines. There was an abortive general strike, but insurrection was kept alive sporadically until 1939, with active propaganda and financial support from Nazi and Fascist sources. The dominant Husseini clan, led by the Mufti, took advantage of the situation to settle accounts with its Arab political opponents, and its gunmen killed more Arabs than Jews.

The British Royal Commission[3] in July 1937 recommended partition of Palestine into Jewish and Arab States, with Jerusalem under perpetual Mandate. The Jews were not opposed to partition on principle, although they recognized that such agreement implied great sacrifice for their aspirations. They held it to be the only solution that would open the doors to Hitler's victims. The Arabs rejected it outright in the belief that the impending Axis victory would enable them to destroy the Jewish community.

Clinging to its policy of appeasement, the Chamberlain Government issued a White Paper in May 1939[4] renouncing the Balfour Declaration and the Mandate on which British authority in Palestine legally rested.

The Jewish population was to be frozen at one-third of the total, and within ten years the country was to become an independent State where the Jews would have a permanent minority status.

The White Paper was rejected by the Arabs, for whom it was "all or nothing." They openly espoused the Axis cause. The Mufti went to Germany where he became a Nazi propagandist and advocated the mass extermination of the Jews. Yet the White Paper was firmly

[3] The Peel Commission. See page 11.
[4] Great Britain, Parliamentary Papers, 1939, Cmd. 6019, pp. 1-12.

applied against the Jews of Palestine, despite the trend of British public opinion and the verdict of the League of Nations Mandates Commission that the policy in it was in contravention of the terms of the Mandate. The Commission had concluded: "From the first, one fact forced itself on the notice of the Commission—namely, that the policy set out in the White Paper was not in accordance with the interpretation which, in agreement with the Mandatory Power and the Council, the Commission had always placed upon the Palestine Mandate."[5]

[5] Report of the Permanent Mandates Commission of the League of Nations on the Policy Laid Down in the (MacDonald) White Paper of May, 1939, made at the 36th Session of the Permanent Mandates Commission, 1939. (Para. 9)

CHAPTER VI

The Second World War: Palestine Jews Contribute to Victory

The Jews of Palestine and the whole world gave their full support to the Allied Powers at the outbreak of war effort. Constituting only 33% of the total population, it contributed 73% of Palestine's volunteers. As a result of Jewish development, Palestine became a major industrial base for the Allied war effort in the World War II. Palestine Jewry mobilized to aid the Middle East. Yet its gates remained shut to hundreds of thousands of Jews who sought entry in flight from Nazi destruction.

THE WHITE PAPER curtailed Jewish immigration to 10,000 each year for the period 1940-45. But because of the serious refugee position an extra 25,000 were to be admitted over that interval. In February 1940 the second anti-Jewish provision of the White Paper came into operation. It drastically restricted land purchases by Jews. The country was divided into three zones. In Zone A, 65% of the whole, no land could be sold by Arabs to Jews. In Zone B (32%), sales required the approval of the High Commissioner. In the minuscule Zone C, only, Jews were at liberty to buy. This, in effect, penned Jewish development into already crowded urban areas.

The Palestine Jewish community and the Zionist movement throughout the world responded to the restriction on immigration by organizing "illegal" entry. In view of the illegality of the White Paper itself, the Jews did not feel themselves bound to abide by it. Moreover, clandestine immigration was prompted—and justified—by intolerable conditions in Nazi Europe. It was, however, temporarily halted by the outbreak of war.

In spite of its revulsion from the White Paper, Palestine Jewry offered Britain its full support as soon as the war began. In September 1939, the Jewish Agency for Palestine proposed the formation of a Jewish army in Palestine to aid the British war effort. This was rejected by the Chamberlain Government, which was also reluctant to accept any large number of Palestine Jews as individual volunteers, although 134,000 of the country's Jewish men and women had registered for combat service. Active recruiting of Jews began only after the fall of France in June 1940, and the growing Axis threat to British positions in the Middle East. The Mandatory Administration ruled that the number of Arab and Jewish recruits should be equal. There was, however, a conspicuous dearth of Arab volunteers and this principle of "parity" was dropped. Statistics for March 1944 showed the total number of Palestine volunteers as 32,068 (23,323 Jews; 8,745 Arabs).[1] In addition, 2,000 young Jewish women joined the Women's Army Auxiliary (ATS) and 3,000 men served with other Allied contingents—Greek, Czech and Free French. Many thousands more joined the Home Guard and Settlement Police. Later, the Churchill Government allowed the formation of a special Jewish Brigade Group, which fought with distinction under Jewish insignia in North Africa and Italy.

Besides all this, volunteer detachments of Haganah, which, despite its unqualified support for the Allied war effort, was still not recognized by the Mandatory as a self-defense force, were trained as guerrilla fighters. They helped the Allies to suppress Rashid Ali's pro-Axis revolt in Iraq. In Syria, where the Vichy French Government had taken over, the Haganah acted. When the British military authorities decided to act in Syria they sent across the border from Palestine an advance guard composed of Jews, Australians and New Zealanders. But first it was necessary to ascertain the enemy's strength in Syria, the reaction of the local population and of the French, the type of weapons they possessed, etc. A number of young Jews volunteered for the job, and this group was able to bring back reliable information of great importance.[2] Many Haganah soldiers were dropped as parachutists

1 Abraham Revusky, *op. cit.*, p. 47.
2 "Jewish Palestine Fights Back," Jewish Agency, London, 1946, p. 10.

behind the German lines in occupied Europe on missions of extreme peril. They were in double jeopardy, both as Allied soldiers and as Jews. Many of them, men and women alike, perished.

Arab hostility to the Allies was not limited to Syria and Iraq. Anwar Sadat, one of Abdul Nasser's closest colleagues in the Junta and Egyptian Minister of State, in his book, "Revolt on the Nile," describes Egypt's pro-Axis stand: ". . . I still think that if ill luck had not so dogged our enterprise, we might have struck a quick blow at the British, joined forces with the Axis and changed the course of events." (p. 42) ". . . Egypt did not believe in an Allied victory." (p. 21). "Despite British pressure, Ali Maher refused to declare war on the Axis." (p. 20) "Now we prepared to fight side by side with the Axis to hasten England's defeat." (p. 48).

By virtue of the advanced economy of its Jewish community, Palestine became a major Allied base for troop concentrations and ordnance and a key communications center. Not only were food supplies for the forces augmented through Jewish farming, but Jewish mechanics, industrial workers and technicians played a full part in the war logistics.

David Ben Gurion, then head of the Jewish Agency, summed up the attitude of Palestine Jewry: "We will fight the war as though there was no White Paper: We will fight the White Paper as though there was no war."[3]

Jewish development proceeded at a slower pace because of White Paper constraints. Nevertheless, by the close of the war the irrigated area under mixed farming had doubled and food production had risen by 35%. In 1943 the High Commissioner made public a post-war "development plan." It made no mention of the Jewish National Home. It assumed that no further Jewish immigration would be permitted after the White Paper quotas had been exhausted. It made no provision for industrial growth. The Mandatory Administration began to minimize the Jewish war effort and conducted mass searches in an attempt to disarm the Jews. It became increasingly clear that the end of the war would mean a renewal of the struggle for Jewish immigration.

[3] Barnet Litvinoff, *Ben-Gurion of Israel,* New York, 1954, p. 132.

CHAPTER VII

The United Nations and Palestine

A United States' proposal for immediate admission of 100,000 Jewish refugees to Palestine was rejected by the British Government in 1945, and the United Nations inherited the Palestine Problem in 1947. A special United Nations Committee on Palestine (UNSCOP) proposed partition into independent Jewish and Arab States linked in economic union, with a separate status for Jerusalem. The General Assembly adopted the plan on November 29, 1947 by the required two-thirds majority vote. The Arabs rejected it. The Jews accepted it. The British Government proceeded with plans for withdrawal. The Jews made preparations for statehood. The Arabs organized war to prevent it.

AT THE END of the Second World War, the United Nations inherited the problem of the future of the former League of Nations Mandate for Palestine. In mid-1945, President Truman urged the British Government to admit 100,000 Jewish refugees, tragic remnant of the Nazi slaughter of six million Jews, for whom no other possibility of emigration was open. Late in 1945 a joint Anglo-American Commission reaffirmed the President's recommendation and advised that the White Paper restrictions be altogether removed. The British Government turned a deaf ear. Meanwhile "illegal" immigration continued rapidly and there was growing resistance by Palestine Jewry to the illegal measures of the Mandatory.

By February 1947, the British decided to turn the problem over to the United Nations. They contented themselves with reporting that the Mandate had become "unworkable."

But it was too late to reverse the trend of history. The White Paper had destroyed all basis of confidence. It had encouraged Arab extremism, and the British Government showed no sign of abandoning appeasement of the Arabs despite the favorable conditions allowed by the Axis defeat for a change in policy. The survivors of European Jewry urgently sought escape from the DP camps. Thousands of them were finding sanctuary in Palestine, for all the naval blockade and the measures to repress its Jews. World opinion against Britain's conduct was hardening. The Zionist Organization, recognizing that there was no other way of continuing the development of the National Home, pressed for implementation of its "Biltmore Program," adopted during the war, for independent Jewish statehood in Palestine.[1]

On April 28, 1947, the United Nations appointed a special committee on Palestine (UNSCOP) to hear the three sides involved in the future of Palestine: Jews, Arabs, and British. A Study Committee of eleven nations, none of them a major power, was set up by the General Assembly to examine the UNSCOP findings. It consisted of Australia, Canada, Czechoslovakia, Guatemala, Holland, India, Iran, Peru, Sweden, Uruguay and Yugoslavia. The UNSCOP report,[2] published on August 31, 1947, contained eleven unanimous recommendations. They included demands for the termination of the Mandate and the granting of independence to Palestine at the earliest possible date. During the transitional period to follow, which should be as short as possible, the authority entrusted with the administration and preparation for independence of Palestine was to be responsible to the United Nations. A prior condition to the granting of independence was that the political structure of the States should be basically democratic, that is, representative in character, and that the preservation of the economic unity of Palestine as indispensable to the life and development of the country and its people was to be accepted as a cardinal principle. A majority of seven members voted in favor of a partition of Palestine, providing for the division of the country into independent Jewish and Arab States and a separate status for the city of Jerusalem under United Nations trusteeship. All three were to be linked in an economic union. The minority favored a Federal State.

[1] Biltmore Hotel, New York, May 1942. Conference called by the American Zionist Emergency Council, representing every sector of the Zionist movement.

[2] United Nations Official Records, General Assembly, Second Session, Supp.11, Vols. I-V.

The majority report was adopted by the required two-thirds majority vote[3] (33 to 13, with 10 abstentions) in the General Assembly on November 29, 1947. Those in favor were: Australia, Belgium, Bolivia, Brazil, Byelorussia, Canada, Costa Rica, Czechoslovakia, Denmark, Dominican Republic, Ecuador, France, Guatemala, Haiti, Iceland, Liberia, Luxembourg, Netherlands, New Zealand, Nicaragua, Norway, Panama, Paraguay, Peru, Philippines, Poland, Sweden, Ukraine, South Africa, Uruguay, U.S.S.R., United States, Venezuela. Those against were: Afghanistan, Cuba, Egypt, Greece, India, Iran, Iraq, Lebanon, Pakistan, Saudi Arabia, Syria, Turkey, Yemen. Those abstaining were: Argentina, Chile, China, Colombia, El Salvador, Ethiopia, Honduras, Mexico, United Kingdom, Yugoslavia. Siam was absent.

THE UNITED NATIONS PARTITION RESOLUTION

"The General Assembly . . . recommends to the United Kingdom, as the Mandatory Power for Palestine, and to all members of the United Nations, the adoption and implementation, with regard to the future Government of Palestine, of the Plan of Partition with Economic Union . . .; Calls upon the inhabitants of Palestine to take such steps as may be necessary on their part to put this plan into effect; Appeals to all Governments and all peoples to refrain from taking any action which might hamper or delay the carrying out of these recommendations. . . ."

(General Assembly Resolution 181 (11) of 29 November 1947)

THIS RESOLUTION envisaged the second partition of Palestine in modern times. The first had taken place in 1921 with the British manufacture of Trans-Jordan, dividing historic Palestine into two territories: in the territory which kept the name of Palestine, only one-fifth was left of the area originally designated for the Jewish National Home. The 1947 resolution meant the reduction of this area further, to 6,000 square miles.

The United Nations resolution could only be implemented if both the Arabs and the Jews accepted it. For it called for the setting up of an independent Jewish state, an independent Palestine Arab state, and an international enclave around Jerusalem, all three parts to be linked in economic union. It was thus an integral resolution.

[3] General Assembly, Second Session, A/P.V. 128, 29 November 1947.

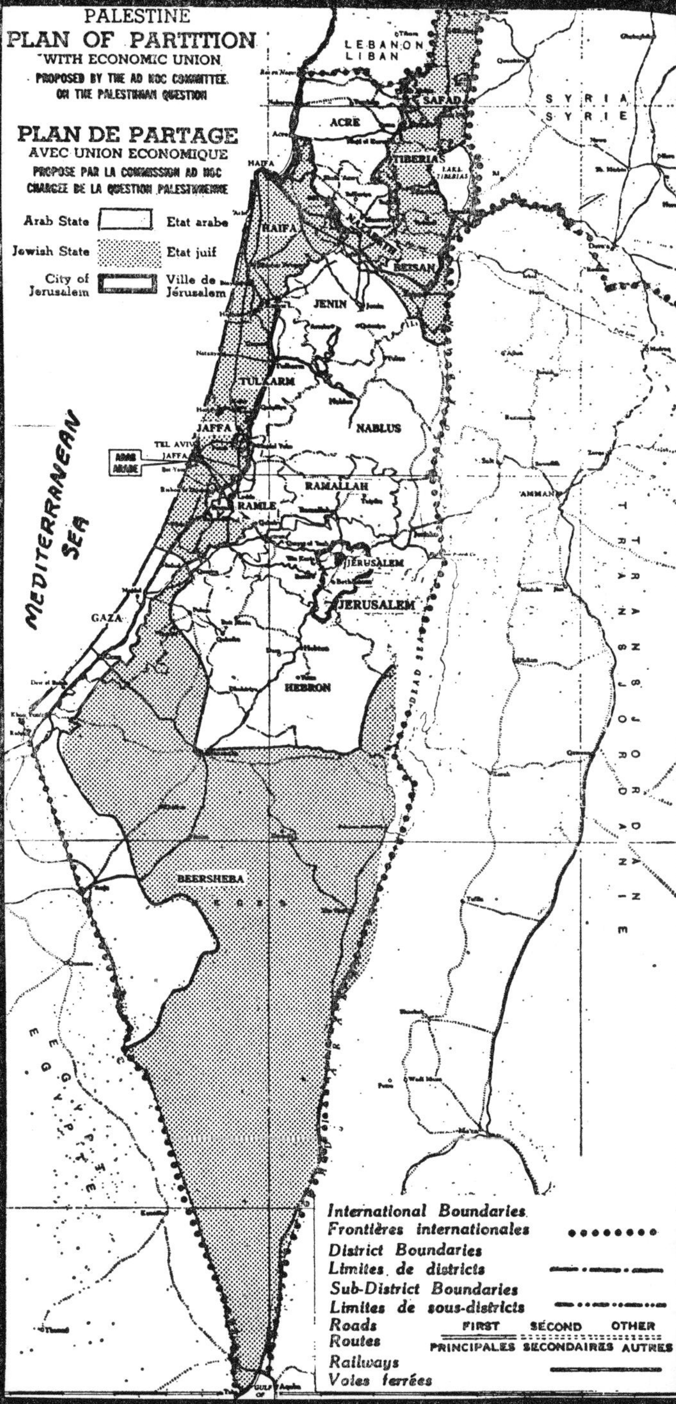

United Nations Palestine Partition Resolution, 29 November 1947:
Map of Proposed Jewish and Palestine Arab States.

Failure to implement any of its parts would obviously mean failure for the whole. Moreover, the partition of Mandatory Palestine envisaged by the resolution was to be between Palestine Jewry and the Palestine Arab community. The Arab States had no claim to an inch of the territory of Mandatory Palestine and the resolution depended for its implementation upon the cooperation of the Jewish and Arab inhabitants of Palestine only.

The Jews accepted the resolution as their contribution, and a momentous sacrifice that contribution was, to a peaceful solution of the problem. The Palestine Arabs, represented by their Higher Committee, and supported by the intervention of the surrounding Arab States, refused to accept the resolution and destroyed it by their attempted conquest of the whole of Mandatory Palestine. The moment invading Arab forces from Jordan conquered the territory of Mandatory Palestine they now hold on the west bank of the River Jordan, and Egyptian forces annexed the area of the Gaza Strip, turning their populations into either citizens of Jordan or refugees, the resolution was undone. Moreover, this not only prevented the birth of the Palestine Arab State which was to have been linked in economic union with Israel but also the establishment in Jerusalem and its environs of an international enclave which, too, was to have been linked in economic union with the independent Jewish and the independent Palestine Arab states. What, in fact, happened was the expansion of Jordan by conquest at the expense of the Palestine Arab State-to-be and a similar expansion by Egypt into the Gaza Strip, both acts in direct violation of the United Nations resolution and hence of the decision of over two-thirds of the world organization. As subsequent events showed, the United Nations was unable to enforce its decision because of the political, and then the military, opposition of Jordan, Egypt, Iraq, Saudi Arabia, Lebanon, Syria and Yemen—the first attempt, unhappily successful, to thwart the implementation of a United Nations decision by force and sabotage the moral authority of the world organization created as an outcome of World War II to be mankind's major instrument of peace.

The partition plan provided for the establishment of a Palestine Arab State to include Western Galilee, the hill country of Samaria and Judaea (excluding Jerusalem), and the coastal plain from Isdud (Ashdod) to the Egyptian frontier. The Jewish State was to comprise Eastern Galilee, the Esdraelon Plain (Emek), most of the coastal plain and the Negev. This meant that each State was split into three sections, linked at three points.[4]

In Jerusalem, the resolution provided for a United Nations trusteeship of Holy Places and minorities. The city was to be demilitarized and ingress and egress were to be free to all.

The economic union for the two States and Jerusalem was to include common currency, communications, postal services, seaports and airports, access to water and power, and joint economic development.

The weakness of the plan was apparent. The boundaries were artificial. Provisions for economic union did not envisage the development on which further Jewish immigration turned. Jerusalem was completely surrounded by Arab territory and had no communications under its own control with the sea. The success of economic union demanded good will and active cooperation between Arabs and Jews. These did not exist.

Rabbi Abba Hillel Silver, on behalf of the Executive of the Jewish Agency and spokesman for Palestine Jewry and the World Zionist Movement, accepted the United Nations resolution. He said: "If heavy sacrifice is the inescapable condition of a final solution, if it makes possible the immediate reestablishment of the Jewish State, the ideal for which a people has ceaselessly striven, then the Jewish Agency is prepared to recommend the acceptance of the partition solution. This sacrifice would be the Jewish contribution to the solution of a painful problem and would bear witness to the Jewish people's spirit of international cooperation and its desire for peace,"[5] although it was a solution that offered considerably less than the original limits of territory and opportunity for development which the Jews believed had been secured to them under the League of Nations Mandate.

On the other hand, the Arabs intransigently opposed the resolution and threatened war to prevent its being carried out.

ARAB OPPOSITION TO UNITED NATIONS RESOLUTION

Arab representatives at the United Nations went on record against partition in the following terms:[6]

[4] See Partition Map on page 31.

[5] United Nations Official Records, General Assembly, Second Session, Summary Records of Meetings, 25 September - 25 November 1947, pp. 16-17.

[6] General Assembly, Second Session, A/P.V. 128, 29 November, 1947; also United Nations Official Records, General Assembly, Second Session, Summary Records of Meetings, 25 September - 25 November 1947.

Mahmoud Fawzi (present Egyptian Foreign Minister): "The decision for partition is not within the scope of the Charter; the delegation of Egypt therefore reserves its right to consider the decision null and void."

Dr. Fadhil Jamali (later Prime Minister of Iraq): "Iraq does not recognize the validity of this decision, and will reserve freedom of action towards its implementation."

Adel Arslan, Syria: "My country will never recognize this proposed partition and we reserve the right to act accordingly."

Camile Chamoun (later President of Lebanon): "This plan is unjust and inequitable. It is a precedent fraught with very serious consequences."

Emir Feisal, Saudi Arabia: "The Government of Saudi Arabia registers on this historic occasion that it considers itself unbound by the resolution . . . It reserves to itself the full right to act freely in whatever way it deems fit."

Prince Seif el Islam Abdullah, Yemen: "The partition plan is illegal . . . The plan is unworkable. The Arabs do not agree to it."

The Arab Premiers, meeting in Cairo on December 9, 1947, declared they would "do everything possible to bring about the collapse of the United Nations partition plan."

The UN resolution had appealed to all Governments and all peoples to refrain from taking any action which might hamper or delay the carrying out of the partition plan. Special obligations were placed upon Britain, as Mandatory, to evacuate the country not later than February 1, 1948, and provide a seaport and hinterland for Jewish immigration; to turn the Administration of the country over to the UN Palestine Commission as evacuation took place; and to take no action to prevent or delay implementation of the resolution.

But Ernest Bevin, British Foreign Secretary, announced, on December 11, 1947, that the Mandate would terminate on May 15, 1948, and British evacuation would be completed by August 1.[7] No facilities were given to the Palestine Commission to operate effectively. It must not arrive until a fortnight before the Mandate ended. The immigration quota would not be increased. Britain would not take part in any collective effort to enforce the UN resolution.

The result in Palestine was anarchy and chaos. The Arabs were encouraged to believe that they could now proceed overtly to undo

[7] Harry Sacher, *Israel: The Establishment of a State,* British Book Centre, New York, 1952, p. 100.

the resolution, with British connivance or acquiescence. The High Commissioner admitted:[8] "The Arabs were firmly convinced that our armed forces were on their side." Eight hundred Arabs from Syria entered Palestine to attack Jewish settlements. A similar number crossed over from Jordan and encamped in Samaria, setting up a local government at Nablus. The Mandatory did nothing to prevent these incursions or to expel the invaders, save place an embargo on the supply of arms to either side. Arms, however, continued to be sent by Great Britain to Arab States in fulfillment of treaty obligations.

The General Assembly had appointed a Palestine Commission of representatives of Bolivia, Czechoslovakia, Denmark, Panama and the Philippines. Its first report to the Security Council, on February 2, 1948, complained that the Mandatory had declined to institute a transfer of authority, withheld provision for a port for Jewish immigration, and denied the Commission the right—and protection—to enter Palestine a reasonable time before the transfer of authority.

It also stated that "powerful Arab interests, both inside and outside Palestine are defying the resolution of the General Assembly and are engaged in a deliberate effort to alter by force the settlement envisaged therein."[9]

When the Security Council met on February 24, faced with Arab opposition and warfare there were hints of retreat and the possibility of relinquishing the General Assembly plan. Moshe Sharett (later Israel's first Foreign Minister), representing the Jewish Agency, told the Council that the Jews of Palestine would stand firm, and "no reduction of Jewish rights either in territory or in sovereignty would be accepted by the Jewish people."[10]

THE JEWS OF PALESTINE PREPARE FOR STATEHOOD

The situation steadily deteriorated, but Palestine Jewry was starting its own course. Faced with local Arab attacks, invasion by infiltrating bands, and anarchy in the country produced by the policy of the Mandatory, on March 23, 1948, the Executive of the Jewish Agency and the Jewish National Council issued a declaration proclaiming that the Jewish people would oppose any proposal to prevent or

[8] Harry Sacher, op. cit., p. 101.

[9] First Special Report to SC by UN Palestine Commission. A/AC.21/9 16 February, 1948.

[10] S.C.O.R. 3rd year, 253rd meeting, 24 February 1948 (No. 16).

postpone the establishment of a Jewish State; that they rejected proposals for a trusteeship regime (then canvassed as an alternative to partition), which would entail denial of Jewish rights to national independence; that the United Nations Commission should proceed to Palestine without delay and recognize a Jewish Provisional Council of Government, so that authority might be transferred to it; that on the termination of the Mandate, and not later than May 16, a Provisional Jewish Government would begin to function in cooperation with UN representatives then in Palestine, and would meanwhile attempt to minimize the chaos caused by the present Government; that the Jewish people extended the hand of peace to the Arab people, and the Jewish State would be glad to cooperate with neighboring Arab States, and to enter into permanent treaty relations with them to strengthen world peace and advance the development of all the countries of the Middle East.

As the Mandate dragged to an end, the Jewish leaders began to form their own organs of Government. The Zionist General Council met in Tel Aviv, from April 6-12, and set up a National Council consisting of elected representatives of the World Zionist Movement resident in Palestine, executives of the Jewish National Council in Palestine (Vaad Leumi), and representatives of other public bodies. Provision was made to grant representation to Arabs in the area of the Jewish State. Plans were framed to float a National Loan, and manpower and supply services were stabilized. Palestine Jewry was ready to take over.

Hampered by the obstructionism and warfare of the Arabs, the United Nations was powerless to act. At midnight on May 14, 1948, the British High Commissioner left Palestine. At that moment the State of Israel was formally proclaimed. It was immediately recognized *de facto* by the United States, whose example was quickly followed by major countries, including the Soviet Union and most of the Western powers.

CHAPTER VIII

The Arab War Against Israel

(1947-1949)

The Arab war against the implementation of the United Nations resolution and the establishment of Israel fell into three main phases:

1. The Arabs organized riots and military action against the Jewish population on November 30, 1947, the day after the UN partition resolution was passed. The "Arab Army of Liberation," trained in Syria, occupied large areas of Palestine. Full-scale Arab invasion began before the establishment of the Jewish State. Jerusalem was besieged. The Jews hastily organized defense measures to re-open communications between Jerusalem and the coast.

2. Five Arab armies invaded Israel on May 15, 1948, the day after the establishment of the new State. The Arab war aim was "extermination and momentous massacre" of the Jews.[1] *After initial successes the Arabs were halted. Under cover of the first UN truce (June 11-July 8), they reinforced their armies to renew the offensive. Failure of their offensive led to the second truce, on July 18. Continued Arab violations of the truce brought about renewed hostilities, ending on January 7, 1949, after an Egyptian defeat in the Negev and Sinai.*

3. Egypt, Jordan, Lebanon, and Syria signed Armistice Agreements with Israel at Rhodes under UN auspices. These agreements were designed as interim measures "promoting the return to permanent peace in Palestine,"[2] *and providing that there should be no change in boundaries at the termination of hostilities, except by mutual consent of the parties.*

1. THE WAR BEFORE THE ESTABLISHMENT OF THE STATE OF ISRAEL

Arab hostilities against the Jewish population of Palestine spread immediately after the General Assembly resolution of November 29, 1947. Widespread violence ensued. The "New York Times" reported from Jerusalem:

> "Jerusalem, November 30—In a violent Arab retort to the U.N. decision on Palestine, seven Jews were killed by Arab ambushes in Palestine today. Five were slain in an attack on one bus and one in an ambush on another bus. Eight passengers in two vehicles were injured. A Jew was also found killed in the Arab city of Jaffa . . . The Palestine Arab Higher Committee, following two sessions, today issued a call to all Arabs of Palestine for a three day general strike beginning Tuesday (December 2) to be followed by mass demonstrations . . . The Arabs will wage a holy war if an attempt is made to enforce the Partition Plan, Dr. Hussein Khalidi, Acting Chairman of the Palestine Arab Higher Committee, declared in an interview tonight . . . Partition, Dr. Khalidi said 'is going to lead to a "crusade" against the Jews'." ("New York Times," December 1, 1947, p. 1.)

By the end of the week 105 Jews had been killed and a large number wounded ("The New York Times," December 7) in Arab attacks in Jerusalem, Jaffa, Haifa, Safad, Ramleh, on the Tel Aviv-Jerusalem road, on the Haifa-Tel Aviv highway, in Jewish settlements in the Galilee, the Hebron area, the Sharon and the Negev, in the Jewish quarter of the Old City of Jerusalem, and on the Jaffa fringe of Tel Aviv. (See too "New York Times" dispatches on December 1, 2, 3, 4, 5, 6, 7.)

December 9: Arab attacks at Haifa;

December 11: Arabs attack Jewish convoys near Kfar Etzion settlements;

December 12: Nine Jews killed in second convoy attack; Arabs kill five Jews near Beersheba;

December 13: Fourteen Jews killed near Lydda.

[1] B.B.C. News Broadcast of May 15, 1948.
[2] Article 1.

Arab strategy was to occupy high ground dominating the main roads and so control all communications. Main targets were the Tel Aviv-Jerusalem and the Jerusalem-Hebron highways.

Within a few weeks, the Arab League Governments began to organize armed intervention. A secret meeting of the Arab League in Sofar in the Lebanon, on September 19, decided to send troops into Palestine if partition was agreed upon by the United Nations.[3] Damascus became the training center for the so-called "Arab Army of Liberation." Syrian officers trained "volunteers," commanded by Fawzi Kaukji, an Arab soldier of fortune. Large detachments infiltrated into Palestine, and by the beginning of March, seven detachments, totalling 5,000 men, had made their way in.

The Arab Invasion Begins

The first armed Arab invasion of Palestine began on January 9, 1948, four months before the termination of the Mandate and the establishment of the State of Israel. A force of 600 uniformed irregulars attacked Jewish settlements in the northeast. They were repelled and withdrew. In February Kaukji's army opened an offensive in the Beisan Valley. His plan was to force an entry into the Valley of Jezreel and move into Haifa. His initial assault failed, and it was not until early April that he was able to mount a second offensive aimed at Mishmar Ha'emek, which controlled the Haifa road. The battle lasted from 4 to 10 April; the defenders held their positions, and the arrival of Haganah reinforcements dispersed the attack. This was the first time Haganah had operated in battalion strength.

At this stage of hostilities, the Jews were unable to use their manpower fully because of lack of weapons; this was due to the British naval blockade. The first large consignment of arms to reach them came from Czechoslovakia, a purchase from the democratic Benes-Masaryk Government. Haganah also began production of small arms, mortars, and ammunition in secret workshops. These were urgently needed, for the situation of the Jewish community was growing more grave as the Arab campaign of assassination and terror reached its peak. As mentioned, the first special report by the UN Palestine Commission, on February 16, had declared:

> "Powerful Arab interests, both inside and outside Palestine, are defying the resolution of the General Asembly and are engaged

[3] Prof. B. Y. Boutros-Gali, University of Cairo: "The Arab League" (International Conciliation No. 498, May 19, 1954, p. 411).

in a deliberate effort to alter by force the settlement envisaged therein."[4]

In March 1948, Jerusalem was besieged and bombarded by Arab Legion forces. On May 12, the Legion launched an attack with tanks and heavy guns on the Etzion group of Jewish villages south of Jerusalem, killing 160 men and women.

A convoy from Jerusalem, which had taken supplies to the besieged Etzion group, was ambushed on March 27 on its return journey near Nebi Daniel, a deserted Arab village. In an unequal battle, some 200 against 3,000, which lasted until the British decided to intervene only to negotiate a Jewish surrender, the Jews lost more than 40 and almost the entire fleet of their armored cars in the Jerusalem area.

In the first phases of the Arab onslaught, the Jews were compelled to depend on convoys to supply outlying settlements. Later, as more weapons became available, they began to capture heights controlling main roads. The Arabs had laid siege to the Jewish quarter of Safad since December with a force of 600 Iraqis and 1,500 local Arabs. Neighboring Jewish settlements were also under attack. The Arabs were in possession, as well, of two police fortresses handed over to them by the British when they abandoned Safad on April 16. Haganah countered with Operation Jephtha on April 18. After a battle which lasted till May 11, the Arab siege was raised and Safad relieved.

During the same week occurred the loss of the convoy to relieve Yechiam with a massacre of 46 Jews.

In another relief operation on April 16, Haganah dispersed a Syrian Druze band which was shelling Jewish settlements on the Tel Aviv-Haifa road. Communications between the Jewish towns of the coast were restored.

Haifa itself was the scene of serious incidents. Arabs massacred 41 Jewish workers at the oil refinery on December 30, 1947. During the following month Syrian and Iraqi troops poured into the city to attack the Jewish suburbs. On April 21, Haganah hit back with an offensive from Mount Carmel. The Arab commanders fled, and General Stockwell, the British commander who was still in the city, arranged a cease-fire. He urged the Arabs to accept Jewish requests for the Arab population to remain. Following is a report by a British eye witness published in the "London Economist" of October 2, 1948:

[4] United Nations Document, A/AC.21/9, 16 February 1948.

"During the subsequent days the Jewish authorities, who were now in complete control of Haifa (save for limited districts still held by British troops), urged all Arabs to remain in Haifa and guaranteed them protection and security. As far as I know, most of the British civilian residents whose advice was asked by Arab friends told the latter that they would be wise to stay. However, of the 62,000 Arabs who formerly lived in Haifa, not more than 5,000 or 6,000 remained. Various factors influenced their decision to seek safety in flight. There is but little doubt that the most potent of the factors were the announcements made over the air by the Arab Higher Executive urging all Arabs in Haifa to quit. The reason given was that on the final withdrawal of the British, the combined armies of the Arab states would invade Palestine and 'drive the Jews into the sea' and it was clearly intimated that those Arabs who remained in Haifa and accepted Jewish protection would be regarded as renegades."

But the Arab leaders spurned the Jewish offer and during a five-day truce the bulk of the Arab population decamped.

The Situation in Jerusalem

Jerusalem was still under siege. More than 100,000 Jews in the New City and 1,700 in the Jewish quarter of the Old City were surrounded by Arabs. Mount Scopus, seat of the Hebrew University and the Hadassah Medical Center, was cut off. The supply situation was alarming. The Arabs controlled the approaches to Jerusalem from Tel Aviv. They also were in a position to interrupt water supplies. They had ambushed numerous Jewish convoys with heavy loss of life.

Haganah launched Operation Nachshon on April 2 to re-open the Tel Aviv highway. This succeeded in part, and food convoys got through until held up again by an Arab counter-offensive.

The Dir Yassin Incident

While Haganah was heavily engaged at Kastel in an effort to dislodge the Arabs from a key position on the Jerusalem-Tel Aviv road, Jewish dissident armed groups, led by the Irgun Zvai Leumi, undertook operations against the village of Dir Yassin, without the cooperation or consent of the main body of the Jewish population organized in Haganah. This village had been for long a nest of Arab snipers and armed bands. The action took place before the establishment of the State of Israel and before effective control by its Government of all armed forces previously engaged in resisting Arab attacks. The incident was unreservedly condemned by all responsible Jewish authorities.

Menachem Beigin, Irgun leader, subsequently stated[5] that Haganah had expressly warned the Irgun command against the attack. He points out, however, that repeated loud-speaker warnings in Arabic advised non-combatants who were killed in the fighting to evacuate the village from which a murderous fire was being directed against the Irgun irregulars.

A prominent inhabitant of the village, Yunes Ahmed Assad, declared:[6]

> "The Jews never intended to hurt the population of the village, but were forced to do so after they met enemy fire from the population, which killed the Irgun commander. The Arab exodus from other villages was not caused by the actual battle but by the exaggerated description spread by Arab leaders to incite them to fight the Jews."

Continuing their offensive on April 13, the Arabs ambushed a Jewish convoy carrying nurses, doctors, and medical supplies to the Hadassah Medical Center. The vehicles were set afire and 77 men and women killed.

In the Old City, the Jewish position had become desperate, but the pious citizens remained quietly in the homes that Jews had occupied for centuries near the site of the Temple. Efforts to arrange a cease-fire were unsuccessful.

The south of the New City, particularly the Katamon district, had been occupied by Iraqi troops who were harassing adjacent Jewish suburbs. The Iraqis were expelled, but the Arabs cut off Jerusalem's water supply.

The Situation at Tel Aviv

During March and April, Iraqi troops, supported by Arab irregulars, opened an attack from Jaffa on Tel Aviv. On April 29, Haganah counter-attacked and two weeks later the Arab city surrendered. There was a see-saw struggle for control of Lydda airport, occupied first by Arabs and then by Jews. On April 27, British troops forced the Jews to withdraw and on their own departure handed the airport over to the Arabs.

[5] M. Beigin "The Revolt," pp. 163-4.

[6] Al Urdun, Jordan, April 9, 1953.

First Phase of Arab War Ends

So concluded the first round of the Arab offensive against the Jews and the UN partition resolution. It was only a prelude to the main invasion. The Syrian-trained "Army of Liberation" had failed in its main objective of seizing control of the greater part of Palestine before the British withdrew. The Arab Legion had wiped out the isolated Jewish settlements of the Etzion bloc. Under Arab fire, Haganah had evolved from a static defense group to the nucleus of an army capable of striking back. It had held Haifa and Eastern Galilee and forced the Arabs to give up their offensive at Jaffa. Arab attempts to break through to the sea had been frustrated. On the other hand, the New City of Jerusalem was under heavy siege.

The Arab offensive had cancelled the boundaries set by the partition resolution. The Arab Commander had encouraged mass departure from towns and villages to free their forces for military operations, promising that early victory would enable the Arab population soon to return and share the spoils of Jewish defeat. They were responsible thereby for the uprooting of hundreds of thousands of their own people.

In a comprehensive analysis of the attitude of the Arab States to the Palestinian refugees, Habib Issa, Acting Editor of Al Hoda, a Lebanese newspaper, wrote on June 8, 1951:

> "The Secretary-General of the Arab League, Abd er-Rahman Azzam Pasha, published numerous declarations assuring the Arab peoples and all others that the occupation of Palestine and of Tel Aviv would be as simple as a military promenade for the Arab armies. Azzam Pasha's statements pointed out that armies were already on the frontiers, and that all the millions that the Jews had spent on land and on economic development would surely be easy booty for the Arabs, since it would be a simple matter to throw the Jews to the bottom of the Mediterranean Sea."[7]

2. AFTER THE ESTABLISHMENT OF THE STATE OF ISRAEL

The Arab Invasion

The war aims of the large-scale invasion of Israel by five Arab armies which began on May 15, 1948, were made plain by Azzam

[7] "The Arab League and the Refugees."

Pasha, then Secretary-General of the Arab League. At a press conference in Cairo on that day, he said:[8]

> "This will be a war of extermination and a momentous massacre which will be spoken of like the Mongolian massacres and the Crusades."

Ahmed Shukairy, today UN Representative of Saudi Arabia, then representative of the Palestine Arab High Committee, added: "The war aims of the Arabs were the elimination of the Jewish State."[9]

King Abdullah assumed the post of Commander-in-Chief of the combined Arab armies in the field.

The Egyptian army, with Saudi Arabian, Sudanese and Yemenite contingents, concentrated on the Palestine frontier with Sinai. It consisted of modern tanks, an artillery regiment, and about 10,000 infantry supported by flights of fighter, bomber and reconnaissance aircraft. The Egyptian plan was for one brigade group to advance along the coast and capture Tel Aviv, while the other would advance through Beersheba and Hebron and link up with the Arab Legion south of Jerusalem, and then storm the city.

The Syrians launched their main attack at Samakh, on the south shore of the Sea of Galilea. A second thrust was aimed at Mishmar Hayarden, south of Lake Hula. The seizure of Nebi Yusha, overlooking the lake, seriously menaced all of Upper Galilee, and imperilled the road to Safad in particular.

The Lebanese forces made an ineffective advance at Malkiya.

The Iraqi army comprised an armored brigade, eight infantry battalions, and three squadrons of aircraft, a total force of 10,000 men. With headquarters at Nablus, in Samaria, they occupied the whole Arab triangle of Nablus-Jenin-Tulkarem, posing a grave hazard to the sea-coast only ten miles away.

At the end of the first six weeks of the fighting, the Egyptians had advanced as far as Isdud (Ashdod) and Bethlehem. The Arab Legion had taken the Jewish quarter of the Old City of Jerusalem, severed communications between Mount Scopus and the New City by capture of Sheikh Jarrah, and cut Jerusalem from Tel Aviv by the occupation of Latrun.

To the south of Jerusalem the Arab Legion had overrun and destroyed the Jewish villages of the Etzion bloc, Revadim, Ein Tzurim,

[8] B.B.C. News Broadcast, May 15, 1948.

[9] First Committee, General Assembly, Official Records, page 650.

Masuot Yitzhak and Kfar Etzion, their survivors taken prisoner. The village of Beit Arava, which had gained renown for its soil desalination and successful cultivation on the shores of the Dead Sea, was overrun and destroyed. Further north of the city, Atarot and Neve Yaakov were captured.

In the north the Lebanese had at length taken Malkiya. The Jewish forces still maintained a largely defensive role: a number of settlements held out in the rear and mobile forces were actively harassing enemy lines.

They had nevertheless substantial grounds for optimism. Such major defeats over the Arab armies as in the battle of the Jerusalem corridor, particularly at Kastel and at Ramat Rachel to the south of the city; the defeat of Kaukji's forces at Mishmar Haemek, and military successes in freeing Tiberias, Safad and Acre of Arab forces, had all given the Jewish defenders not only confidence but also the initial military experience they needed. At the same time high hopes of a speedy victory, originally held by the Arab command, had been dashed to the ground. The Arab offensive ground to a stop..

Disappointed of rapid victory, and the tide of war now beginning to turn against them, the Arabs, after initially resisting United Nations cease-fire appeals, were constrained in the end to accept a truce. It started on June 11 and lasted four weeks.

This first truce prescribed cessation of movement of military materials and forbade reinforcement of armies in the field. Under its cover, Egypt enlarged its army to 18,000 men, including "volunteers" from Sudan, Saudi Arabia and North Africa, called up Spitfires and added to its artillery and mortars. The Iraqi force grew to 15,000. So, during the truce period, the strength of the Arab forces was doubled—from 25,000 to 50,000.[10]

To begin with, the Israelis had only 15,000 men under arms. They could muster only a few artillery pieces. Converted trucks were their only mobile armor. Their airforce comprised a few Piper Cubs for reconnaissance.

Count Folke Bernadotte,[11] the United Nations Mediator, produced terms for an Armistice, which were unacceptable to both sides. The Israelis did, however, agree to a prolongation of the truce. The Arabs

[10] "The Arab-Israeli War 1948," by Edgar O'Ballance (Praeger, N. Y.), p. 137.

[11] On May 14, 1948 the General Assembly adopted a resolution calling for the appointment of a mediator for Palestine, and on May 20, Count Folke Bernadotte, head of the Swedish Red Cross, was named to the position.

decided to renew fighting in the hope this time of achieving swift triumph.

The Ten-Day Offensive

The Egyptians reopened hostilities with an attack on the Jewish settlement of Beer Tuvia on July 8, a day before the truce was due to expire. They were held and driven back. The Israelis went over to the offensive and by July 18 had pushed back the Egyptians in the south. On the central front, they wrested Ramleh and Lydda from the Arab Legion. The Arab Legion held on to Latrun, but to do so was forced to withdraw troops from the siege of Jerusalem. In Galilee, Israel forces defeated Kaukji and took Nazareth. The only Arab gains were by the Syrians at Mishmar Hayarden.

Now truly apprehensive of a military debacle, the Arabs welcomed a second truce on July 18.

Count Bernadotte proposed new terms of final settlement on September 16. Israel proposed, instead, direct negotiations, in a letter addressed by her Foreign Minister, Mr. Moshe Sharett, to the Mediator. The Arab States rejected both the terms of final settlement offered by Count Bernadotte and any direct negotiations proposed by the Israelis.

On September 17, Count Bernadotte was assassinated by members of a dissident military organization refusing to accept the command or discipline of the Haganah, the defense force of the Jewish community. Despite vigilant searches for the perpetrators of the act, universally condemned by the Jewish authorities and population, they were not discovered. One of the first acts of the newly constituted Government of Israel was forcibly to disband the dissident groups, known as the Irgun Zvai Leumi and Stern.

The Egyptian Defeat

The second truce allowed free access for food supplies to Jewish settlements behind Egyptian lines. Egyptian forces unremittingly attacked the convoys and the Israelis took military action to restore communications.

On October 22, Kaukji's army of the north penetrated into Upper Galilee, making some gains. A week later the Israelis drove it out and cleared all Galilee.

The final stages of the war were now at hand. On December 10, an Egyptian force began a new offensive on the Jewish villages of the south and made some headway. The Israelis counter-attacked on December 22. They took El Auja and enveloped the whole Egyptian army by reaching Abu Ageilah, inside the Sinai Peninsula. Britain, which still had a military treaty with Egypt, threatened to intervene, and the Israelis fell back across the old Palestine border. Israel had already agreed to overall armistice talks, pursuant to the Security Council resolution of November 16, 1948. Still sanguine of military success, the Egyptians stalled for a time, until, on January 7, 1949, their reverses in the Negev obliged them to seek an armistice.

The end of the fighting left the Gaza Strip in the hands of Egypt and the area on the west bank of the Jordan River captured by the Arab Legion in the hands of Jordan. The annexation of both of these territories by Egypt and Jordan was in violation of the United Nations partition decision of November 29, 1947, as these territories had been earmarked as part of the designated Palestine Arab State. Their annexation prevented this State from being established and voided the entire United Nations resolution which had envisaged that on the territory of mandatory Palestine an independent Jewish State, an independent Palestine Arab State and an international enclave around Jerusalem would be established in economic union. Obviously no such union could be effected as Jordan refused to hand over the Old City of Jerusalem and the territory on the west bank, whilst Egypt insisted on her continued occupation of the Gaza Strip. Instead of economic union, the Arab States followed up the Armistice Agreements with economic boycott and maritime blockade against Israel and the continuation of the war by other means.

CHAPTER IX

The Armistice Agreements

Designed by their authors as temporary measures to be replaced by permanent Peace Treaties within a short space of time, a series of General Armistice Agreements with Israel were signed under United Nations auspices early in 1949. The Arab States involved were Egypt, Lebanon, Jordan and Syria. Iraq, whose armies had played so large a part in the invasion, declined to sign on the grounds that it had no common frontier with Israel. Saudi Arabia and Yemen, though they contributed no less to the invasion, also refused to sign.

THE ARMISTSCE AGREEMENTS, of which that between Egypt and Israel, signed at Rhodes on February 24, 1949, was the prototype,[1] laid special emphasis on a number of governing principles:

ARTICLE I: (3) Guaranteed the right of each party to security and freedom from fear of attack by the armed forces of the other.

(4) Explicitly declared that the Armistice was "accepted as an indispensable step towards the liquidation of armed conflict and the restoration of peace in Palestine."

ARTICLE II: (2) Laid down that "no element of the land, sea, or air military or para-military forces of either party, including non-regular forces, shall commit *any warlike or*

[1] See Appendix.

hostile act against the military or para-military forces of the other party, or against civilians in territory under the control of that party."

ARTICLE VII: (1) Again expressed the intention of the parties "to eliminate the threat to peace in Palestine and facilitate the transition from the present truce to permanent peace."

ARTICLE XII: (3) Authorized either of the parties to call upon the United Nations Secretary-General to convoke a conference of representatives of the two parties for the purpose of reviewing, revising or suspending any of the provisions of the Agreement. Participation in this conference was to be obligatory.

(4) If the conference did not result in an agreed solution of matters in dispute, either party could bring them before the Security Council "for the relief sought, on the grounds that the Agreement was concluded in pursuance of Security Council action toward the end of achieving peace in Palestine."

The Armistice Agreements, in reality, represented non-aggression pacts between the parties and invested the exact borders between Israel and the Arab States with the character and legality of an international frontier by requiring that they could only be changed by mutual consent.

THE PALESTINE CONCILIATION COMMISSION AND LAUSANNE

The Armistice Agreements, concluded at the beginning of 1949, were but one part of a two-fold effort under UN auspices to end the Arab-Israel conflict. The second effort, more ambitious in scope, sought to establish lasting peace between Israel and her neighbors. It was assigned by the United Nations to a Palestine Conciliation Commission of three men representing the United States, France and Turkey, which the General Assembly set up at its meeting in Paris in December 1948.

The Palestine Conciliation Commission first sought to bring Arabs and Israelis together around the conference table with the aim of finding common ground upon which a peace settlement could rest. The Arab States adamantly refused to sit with Israel's representatives. Israel, on its part, suggested direct negotiations. The Palestine Conciliation Commission was left with no alternative but to convene two separate meetings, one with each delegation. These were held on May 12, 1949 at Lausanne and each meeting ended with the signing of identical protocols. This was the identical text to which the signatures of the Arab delegations and the members of the Commission, and those of the Israel Delegation and the same members of the Commission were appended in their separate documents:

> "The United Nations Conciliation Commission for Palestine, anxious to achieve as quickly as possible the objectives of the General Assembly resolution of 11 December 1948, regarding refugees, the respect for their rights and the preservation of their property, as well as territorial and other questions, has proposed to the Delegations of the Arab States and to the Delegation of Israel that the working document attached hereto be taken as a basis for discussions with the Commission.
>
> "The interested Delegations have accepted this proposal with the understanding that the exchange of views will be carried on by the Commission with the two parties which will bear upon the territorial adjustments necessary to the above indicated objectives.
>
> Lausanne, May 12, 1949."

The "working document" referred to in the first paragraph was the partition map annexed to the General Assembly resolution of November 29, 1947.

The protocols were neither "an agreement" nor "a covenant" between Israel and the Arab States, or between them, respectively, and the Commission, to implement specific solutions to problems of boundaries, the internationalization of Jerusalem or any other matter in dispute. They were simply an agreement to discuss, to negotiate; each party reserving the right to state its own position. The outstanding aspect of the protocols is the mutual recognition of each other's formal, legal, sovereign existence by the parties. The authorized representatives of Egypt, Jordan, Lebanon and Syria there and then signed an international document which referred "to the Delegations of the Arab States and to the Delegation of Israel" as recognized political entities having equal international status. The 1947 partition map, referred to as the working document, was attached "as a basis for discussion with the Commission" in which each party would preserve its right to state its own position in regard to that "basis." At the time the protocols were signed, this map was the only official UN document that could have been used as a basis for discussions. On 12 May 1949 only three Armistice Agrements had yet been signed—between Israel and Egypt, Israel and Jordan and Israel and Lebanon. Their endorsement by the Security Council in August 1949 only took place after the fourth Agreement between Israel and Syria had been signed in July, 1949.

The Commission *ab initio* looked upon the protocols as a mere request extended to it by the parties to facilitate negotiations on a certain basis. When it failed to reduce the difference between the rival claims, its Acting Chairman advised the General Assembly at its Fifth Session in 1950 that "he doubted whether it (the protocols) could serve as a basis for negotiations at the present time."[2] Subsequently, the Commission convened the Paris Conference in September-October 1951 for negotiations with the Delegations, and submitted to them a "comprehensive pattern of proposals" for reaching a settlement of the Arab-Israel dispute.[3] The proposals dealt with territorial adjustments, refugees, war damages, etc. and contained no reference whatsoever to the protocols or the "working document" attached to them.

In the light of the Armistice Agreements, which were concluded in July 1949 and endorsed by the Security Council the following month, the basis for discussions envisaged in the protocols had changed with the emergence of new legal and factual developments. Israel adhered, and still adheres, to the main purpose of the Lausanne protocols, however, a peaceful and negotiated settlement with the Arab States.

Unfortunately, the Arab States have not. Ten years have passed since the protocols were initialed and the Armistice Agreements, which superseded them as a basis for discussion, were signed. But no Peace Treaties have yet been drawn up because of the refusal of the Arab States to negotiate directly with Israel. Between November 1953 and May 1954, Israel repeatedly invoked Article XII (3) against Jordan, calling for such negotiations but Jordan flatly and flagrantly repudiated its obligations under that provision, and the

[2] United Nations Document A/AC/385R.70, par. 11.

[3] 10th Progress Report of U.N. Conciliation Commission for Palestine, Doc. A/1985, par. 23.

Security Council was powerless to enforce its compliance with the terms of an international contract to which it had solemnly subscribed.[4]

Israel has repeatedly drawn attention to the fact that the Armistice Agreements were meant as transitional steps towards permanent peace, and has since volunteered time and again to enter into negotiations for that purpose. The Arab States have consistently declined.

In successive attempts to bridge the gap between Armistice Agreements and permanent peace, Israel in the last eleven years has made, unilaterally, a series of offers to the Arab States. To mention but a few of these, the Israel Delegation at the Paris Conference of the Palestine Conciliation Commission, on September 21, 1951, proposed a non-aggression pact; on November 4, 1951, Israel offered to negotiate compensation to Arabs who abandoned their land and dwelling places in Israel; in a statement before the Knesset (parliament) by Mr. Moshe Sharett, Minister for Foreign Affairs; on April 10, 1953, the Israel Government announced its decision to release accounts held by Arab refugees in Israel banks; on September 17, 1954, Mr. Moshe Sharett, then Prime Minister as well as Minister for Foreign Affairs, in an interview with a correspondent of "U.S. News and World Report," offered Jordan free port facilities at Haifa as part of a peace settlement with that country; on September 25, 1954, in an Arabic broadcast over Israel's official broadcasting station, Kol Israel, Mr. Gideon Rafael, Counselor in Charge of Middle Eastern Affairs in the Israel Ministry for Foreign Affairs, expressed his country's willingness to serve as a bridge between the Arab States, offering a land passage across her territory.

Between 1954 and the present time offers of peace by Israel, in various forms, partial or total, have again and again been reiterated by its responsible leaders and spokesmen. On September 24, 1959, in a statement at the fourteenth session of the United Nations General Assembly, Mrs. Golda Meir, Israel Minister for Foreign Affairs, stated:

[4] On November 23, 1953, on the request of Israel, Mr. Dag Hammarskjold, Secretary-General of the United Nations, sent a telegram to the Minister of Foreign Affairs of Jordan, involking Article XII (S/3911). On November 24, 1953, a Security Council resolution assumed such a conference would take place. On February 18, 1954, the Secretary-General again attempted, on Israel's initiative, to invoke Article XII. The Jordanian Government persistently refused to honor the Article, and on March 24, 1954, Mr. Hammarskjold wrote to Mr. Abba Eban, Israel's Permanent Representative at the United Nations: "I consider, that for the present my pursuance of this matter any further is not warranted" (S/3180/add.1).

"The sterile conflict between our neighbors and ourselves creates an unhappy and dangerous situation not only for us but for them, too, and for the world at large. We seek nothing from them but the chance to live in amity, and together with them to develop our region for the common good of all who inhabit it . . . Israel believes in a future of peace and cooperation in the area."

On November 13, 1959, the London "Times" published a despatch from its correspondent in Tel Aviv following an interview with Mr. Ben Gurion. The despatch stated:

"Mr. Ben Gurion said he would offer the Arabs complete disarmament in the Middle East with mutual inspection, and if they were not yet ready for peace and complete cooperation, Israel would offer them political, economic and cultural relations, and a non-aggression pact."

On that same date Mr .Michael Comay, Israel's Representative at the United Nations, stated in a speech before the Special Political Committee:

"We would repeat most solemnly that Israel seeks nothing from its neighbors but the chance to live in peace with them and together with them to strive for the common good of our troubled region. To promote this not unworthy end, we repeat that we would be willing to meet with Arab representatives at any time and place, publicly or privately, and without any prior conditions whatsoever. Despite every discouragement we cling to this vision of peace and progress for their people and ours, based on respect for each other's political independence and territorial integrity."

These and innumerable other peace offers to negotiate, directly or indirectly, of summit conferences on neutral territory, of non-aggression pacts in various forms, of cooperation on various practical levels, all met with either scorn or absolute silence from each and all of the Arab States. In fact, in response, these offers often provoked the reaction that "Israel is attempting to trap us (the Arab States) into making peace with her." This view is most succinctly expressed in such statements as:

"The Armistice Agreements are a means of bringing about the second round, while Israel hopes that these Agreements will act as a bridge towards healing Arab wounds and a possible peace."

Al Jihad, Jordan daily, Sept. 11, 1955.

"In the last analysis the difference between peace and unrest in our region depends upon Israel's annihilation. Any agreement based on this thesis will not be final, but merely equivalent to a 'second truce'. The problem is not one of merely reshaping the borders in this or that place but is basically, and stands before us, the elimination of Israel."

Al Akhbar, Egyptian daily, March 22, 1956.

ARAB AIM TO EXTERMINATE ISRAEL

A return to the *ipsissima verba* of the 1947 resolution, especially its boundary provisions, is occasionally propounded by Arab propagandists as the preliminary condition of a settlement with Israel. When they do so, reference is usually made to the Lausanne protocols as "an agreement" by Israel to accept the 1947 boundaries rather than as a "basis for discussion" immediately superseded by the Armistice Agreements themselves. No offer is at the same time made by the Arabs to withdraw from territory occupied on the west bank of the Jordan or the Gaza Strip, or from the Old City of Jerusalem which, according to the same 1947 resolution, were to have been a part of the Palestine Arab State and internationalized Jerusalem. How disingenuous these spokesmen are is revealed by the candid admission of a former Egyptian Foreign Minister:

"It is neither right nor honorable for Arab statesmen to hide behind diplomatic answers that they cannot consider peace with Israel until it implements the UN resolution," said Dr. Mohammed Salah Ed-Din. "The Arab peoples," he confessed, "are not afraid to disclose that they will not be satisfied with anything less than the obliteration of Israel from the map of the Middle East" (Al Misri, Cairo daily, April 11, 1954).

His words are borne out not only by the immediate reaction of the Arab States to the partition resolution, as well as by consistent Arab policies since then, aimed at the dismemberment of Israel. They are also emphasized by statements made *before* the UN decision of 20 November 1947.

Delegates of other neighboring Arab States made declarations to the same effect. And in 1955, Major Salah Salem, a member of the Egyptian Cabinet at that time, stated:

"Egypt will strive to erase the shame of the Palestine War, even if Israel should fulfil the United Nations resolution; it will not sign a peace treaty with her even if Israel should consist only of Tel Aviv."[5]

[5] "Manchester Guardian," January 28, 1955.

But the consideration which conclusively nullifies a return to the boundary provisions of the 1947 resolution is the fact that those provisions were voided and undone by Arab aggression.

The resolution had been conceived in terms of a peaceful compromise, in the spirit of the UN Charter, between conflicting claims of Arabs and Jews. The invasion of Israel by the Arab States, when Israel proclaimed its independence in fulfilment of the UN decision, set that basic condition at naught and the aftermath of the invasion blotted out the territorial definitions which the resolution had conditionally framed.

The 1949 Armistice Agreements between Israel and Egypt, Jordan, Lebanon and Syria respectively, as binding and international contracts validated by the Security Council, thereupon superseded the territorial definitions of the resolution. The demarcation lines which constitute an integral part of those Agreements are subject to change only by mutual consent of the parties concerned. That requirement has in fact made the armistice lines into international boundaries, in the light of the rule of international law that no border between two States may be altered except by their common agreement.

The Arabs, having aggressively destroyed the 1947 resolution, cannot resurrect it in 1959; they cannot reprobate it then and approbate it now.

CHAPTER X

The Arab War Against Israel Since 1949

The Arab States have repeatedly and systematically violated the Armistice Agreements with Israel, voluntarily signed under UN auspices in 1949, which were intended "to facilitate the transition to permanent peace in Palestine."

ARAB AGGRESSIONS AGAINST ISRAEL continued by land through shelling, military incursions, and infiltration of fedayeen, irregular and terrorist forces, causing over 1,300 Israel casualties (1949-1956) and millions of dollars worth of damage to property.[1] Israel's countermeasures were invariably in retort to Arab provocations. Arab land violations diminished after Israel eliminated Egypt terrorist bases in the Sinai campaign of 1956.

The Egyptian Government imposed a maritime blockade on Israel during the 1948-49 invasion, denying legal right of passage

[1] Casualties sustained by Israel as a result of incursions and bombardment by Egyptian military and para-military forces across the Gaza Strip and Sinai borders, mostly among the civilian population, totaled 465 dead and wounded by summer of 1956. These figures were given by Ambassador Abba Eban in a statement before the First Emergency Special Session of the United Nations General Assembly on November 1, 1956. On April 8, 1956, General Burns, the United Nations Chief of Staff, addressed a letter to the Foreign Minister of Israel which stated: "I will despatch to the Prime Minister of Egypt a protest against the action of the fedayeen, assuming it to have been authorized or tolerated by the Egyptian authoriies, and requesting the immediate withdrawal of any persons under Egyptian control from the territory of Israel. . . . I consider that if Egypt has ordered these fedayeen raids she has now put herself in the position of the aggressor."

Security Council Official Records—4th year, 434th meeting, 4 Aug. 1949 (No. 36)

to Israel ships and vessels of other nations bound to and from Israel ports through the Suez Canal and the Gulf of Akaba. The Akaba blockade was lifted in 1956 after the Sinai campaign. The Egyptians still maintain their illegal Suez blockade, which has been condemned on several occasions by the United Nations.

The Arab States have prolonged their war of aggression against Israel by economic boycott, blacklisting of foreign merchants dealing with Israel and blackmailing pressures on traders.

The Armistice Agreements of 1949, as understood by their sponsors and signatories, were intended as transitional steps towards permanent peace, and it was not believed that their life would be longer than a few months.

The Security Council confirmed the armistice lines in its endorsement of the Agreements on August 11, 1949. The Arab States and Israel undertook thereunder to terminate irrevocably all acts of hostility and to advance towards a final peace settlement.

The Arab Delegations which signed the Agreements were fully aware of their consequent obligations. The present Egyptian Foreign Minister, Mahmoud Fawzi, then Egyptian Delegate to the Security Council, declared at its meeting on August 4, 1949:

> "We heard the United Nations Acting Mediator (Dr. Ralph Bunche) say that these Armistice Agreements are tantamount to a non-aggression pact. We heard the distinguished spokesman of Israel say that they are a provisional settlement which can only be supplemented by a peace settlement, and that the Agreements have no time limit. As to the question of Palestine, the Armistice Agreements concerning it are bound in unequivocal assurances and commitments not to resort to force and even plan or threaten to resort to force in its settlement."

The Syrian Delegate, Rafiq Asha, added: "My Government did not authorize the signing of the Armistice Agreement until it had examined every provision most carefully. The Government of Syria honors its words and fully respects agreements into which it enters."[2]

Thereupon the Arab States proceeded, singly and jointly, to demonstrate that these professions of good faith had no substance, and were merely contrived to veil continued aggression against Israel.

After the breakdown of the efforts of the UN Palestine Conciliation Commission to arrange direct negotiations at Lausanne in 1949,

[2] Security Council Official Records—4th year, 434th meeting, 4 Aug. 1949 (No. 36).

the Arab States continued to wage border and guerrilla warfare, economic warfare, maritime blockade, and propaganda war at home and abroad against Israel through the press, radio, pulpit and schoolroom. They initiated an arms race with the openly proclaimed aim of launching a "second round" to destroy Israel. These efforts were intensified with the passing of time. Sporadic infiltration and marauding were sharpened into organized warfare by fedayin terrorist task-groups starting from the Gaza Strip, Sinai, Jordan, Syria and the Lebanon, under Egyptian army direction.

A world-wide economic warfare was waged against Israel with regional boycott offices in Arab States and in their overseas Missions. Boycott by the Arab States did not begin with the end of the war. It was a continuation of Arab policy initiated during the Mandatory period when in 1936 the Palestine Arab Higher Committee began its boycott of the Jewish community in an attempt to starve it into surrender. Propaganda machines engaging in anti-Israel incitement and slander were set up on an international scale, and Arab non-recognition of Israel came to include refusal to attend international conferences at which Israel sat.

The Suez Canal was barred to Israel ships and ships of other nations trafficking with Israel, and Egyptian batteries prevented shipping from passing through the Gulf of Aqaba to and from the Israel port of Eilat. Merchant ships of all countries, loading or unloading at Israel ports, were black-listed and denied facilities in Arab ports or access to them. Blackmailing techniques—exclusion from Arab markets—were exercised against merchants trading or seeking to trade with Israel.

At the same time, Arab preparations to renew the military assault on Israel had reached a point of acute readiness by October 1956, when an Egyptian army equipped with Soviet jets, tanks, and artillery, reinforced by 1,500 fedayin,[3] was about to mount a massive

[3] Fedayin: Egyptian para-military forces, recruited among Palestine Arab refugees in the Gaza Strip and trained by the Egyptian army to raid and terrorize Israel's civilian population. Characteristic actions were the mining of roads, bombing of schools, destruction of water pipelines and installations and ambushing of buses and individuals on highways under cover of darkness. Fedayin units were stationed on Jordanian, Lebanese and Syrian territory, with the agreement of the Governments of these countries to launch their attacks on all fronts either in concert or consecutively. Documents found on fedayin casualties and captured from their headquarters in the Gaza Strip by Israel's army in November 1956 established that the fedayin were created and commanded by official Egyptian armed forces and were not, as initially portrayed by Arab propaganda, a spontaneous and undirected activity of Palestine Arab refugees or Arab citizens. These documents also established the collusion of the Egyptian and other Arab Governments in the conducting of fedayin warfare against Israel across all its borders. Innumerable statements broadcast by the Cairo

offensive for the destruction of Israel. It was frustrated only by the timely counter-measures of the Israel Defense Forces in the Sinai campaign, counter-measures taken because of United Nations' impotence to call a halt to Arab aggression, counter-measures fully consonant with the right of self-defense conferred on all nations by Article 51 of the United Nations Charter.

President Eisenhower in his nation-wide broadcast on the Middle East crisis (October 31, 1956) recognized Egyptian responsibility:

> "We are fully aware of the grave anxieties of Israel, of Britain and France. We know that they have been subjected to grave and repeated provocations."

Israel is not the only country to have been subjected to provocations of this sort, nor is it alone in having had recourse to military counter-actions after all other appeals had proved in vain. Thus, for instance when faced with incursions of Mexican guerrilla forces into American territory in 1916, the United States finally reverted to the despatch of an expeditionary force under General John J. Pershing into Mexico. As Secretary of State Robert Lansing then put it in a note to the Government of Mexico:

> "It would be tedious to recount instance after instance, outrage after outrage, atrocity after atrocity, to illustrate the true nature and extent of the widespread conditions of lawlessness and violence which have prevailed. During the past nine months, in particular, the frontier of the United States along the lower Rio Grande has been thrown into a state of constant apprehension and turmoil because of frequent and sudden incursions into American territory and depredations and murders on American soil by Mexican bandits, who have taken the lives and destroyed the property of American citizens, sometimes carrying American citizens across the international boundary with the booty seized... American ranches have been raided, property stolen and destroyed, and American trains wrecked and plundered . . . Since these attacks, leaders of the bandits well known both to Mexican military and civil authorities as well as to American officers, have been enjoying with impunity the liberty of the towns of northern Mexico. So far has the indifference of the *de facto* Government to these atrocities gone that some of these leaders, as I am advised, have received not only the protection of that Government but encouragement and aid as well . . .

and other State-controlled radios in the Arab countries praising the fedayin as "heroes" and threatening further and larger scale action of this kind against Israel were made almost daily until the Israel defense forces eliminated the fedayin nests in Gaza and Sinai during their operation of October-November 1956.

". . . despite repeated requests by the United States, and without apparent recognition on its (Mexico's) part of the desirability of putting an end to these systematic raids, or of punishing the chief perpetrators of the crimes committed, because they menaced the good relations of the two countries, American forces pursued the lawless bands as far as Parral . . . In this manner and for these reasons have American forces entered Mexican territory . . .

"Obviously, if there is no means of reaching bands roving on Mexican territory and making sudden dashes at night into American territory it is impossible to prevent such invasions unless the frontier is protected by a cordon of troops. No government could be expected to maintain a force of this strength along the boundary of a nation . . . for the purpose of resisting the onslaughts of a few bands of lawless men, especially when the neighboring state makes no effort to prevent these attacks. The most effective method of preventing raids of this nature, as past experience has demonstrated, is to visit punishment or destruction on the raiders. It is precisely this plan which the United States desires to follow along the border without any intention of infringing upon the sovereign rights of her neighbor . . . If the Mexican Government is unwilling or unable to give this protection by preventing its territory from being the rendezvous and refuge of murderers and plunderers, that does not relieve this Government from its duty to take all the steps necessary to safeguard American citizens or American soil. The United States Government cannot and will not allow bands of lawless men to establish themselves upon its borders with liberty to invade and plunder American territory with impunity and, when pursued, to seek safety across the Rio Grande, relying upon the plea of their Government that the integrity of the soil of the Mexican Republic must not be violated....

"The first duty of any government is the protection of life and property. This is the paramount obligation for which governments are instituted, and governments neglecting or failing to perform it are not worthy of the name . . . Protection of American lives and property, then, in the United States is first the obligation of this Government."[4]

Israel's defensive action, following successive but unsuccessful attempts through the United Nations to achieve border peace, disarmed the aggressor, eliminated the fedayin nests and ended the Egyptian sea blockade against Eilat. The blockade of Israel ships, and ships of other nations bound to and from Israel ports in the Suez Canal, is however, still in operation.

[4] Excerpts from Note of the Secretary of State of the United States (Robert Lansing) to the Secretary of Foreign Relations of Mexico, June 20, 1916 . . . Department of State, U.S. Government Printing Office, Washington, 1916.

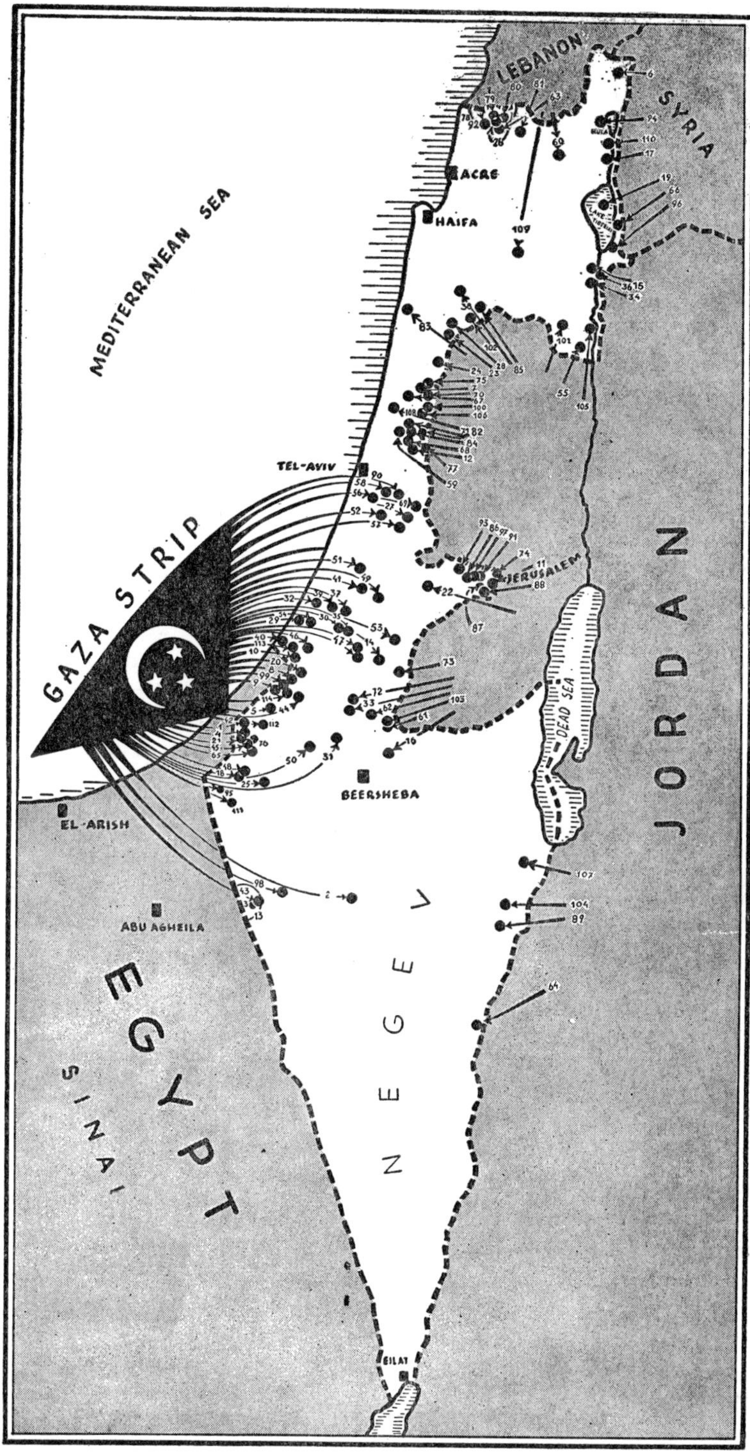

MAP OF ARAB ATTACKS, 1956:

Arrows indicate origin and direction of Arab attacks, preponderantly from Gaza Strip. Armistice frontiers indicated by broken line. Arab territory, including Gaza Strip and Jordan salient—shaded.

ARAB VIOLATIONS BY LAND

Since the signing of the Armistice Agreements in 1949, Israel has been the victim of constant Arab infiltration and rapine and has suffered heavy casualties.

It was not until 1953 that Israel took its first protective action. By that time there had been 7,896 cases of Arab infiltration, sabotage and murder, and 639 Israel casualties. Nevertheless, Israel practiced self-restraint. When she did embark on counter-measures, it was by direct attack on Arab terrorist bases. While over two-thirds of Arab casualties were military or para-military personnel, some four-fifths of the casualties sustained by Israel were civilian.

Between the signing of the Agreements and the Sinai campaign of October 1956, there were 11,873 instances of Arab sabotage and banditry compared with 12 Israel defense actions. There were 1,335 Israel casualties.

By mid-1956 a well-defined pattern of Arab aggression had emerged. The military pacts between the Arab States included arrangements for alternating attacks on Israel from one frontier to another. During the Sinai campaign Egyptian documents were captured proving that Egyptian-trained and commanded fedayin units were transferred from one Arab territory to another.[5]

On every single occasion when the Security Council considered Israel rejoinders to Arab aggression, it has been at pains to point out that incessant Arab infiltrations, sabotage and murder were answerable for Israel's counter-actions. In the "Report by the Chief of Staff of the Truce Supervision Organization Concerning the Incident of February 28, 1955, near Gaza," General Burns stated:

> "Infiltration from Egyptian controlled territory has not been the only cause of present tension, but has undoubtedly been one of its main causes."[6]

The Gaza incident had been the culmination of a long series of Egyptian provocations and acts of aggression. Between September 1, 1954, and February 1, 1955, Egypt was condemned no fewer than 27 times for violations of the Armistice Agreement. On January 21, 1955, an Egyptian army unit crossed the lines and attacked an Israel military post, killing or wounding all its occupants. When this attack was

[5] Directorate of Military Intelligence Office—Palestine, No. 3597/24/1, Gaza 15/8/1956.

[6] United Nations Document S-3373, March 17, 1935.

condemned by the Israel-Egyptian Armistice Commission three days later, this in no way inhibited the Egyptian authorities. The condemnation, in the form of a resolution adopted on January 24, 1955, by the Mixed Armistice Commission, stated in part:

"The Commission finds that . . . an Egyptian military patrol . . . commanded by an officer, attacked an Israel post in Israel, manned by three Israeli soldiers . . . killing one and wounding the other two;

"Notes that the Armistice demarcation line was clearly marked near the place of the attack;

"Decided that this aggressive action carried out by the above mentioned unit of the Egyptian army commanded by an officer is a flagrant violation of Article II, para. 2, of the General Armistice Agreement by Egypt;

"Notes with extremely grave concern this aggressive action, and calls upon the Egyptian authorities to terminate these aggressive acts against Israel."[7]

Three days later, an Egyptian armed band attacked the settlement of Ein Hashlosha and ambushed its farmers. On January 27, 1955, the Mixed Armistice Commission again developed its condemnation of Egypt into a generalized criticism:

"Notes with grave concern the serious situation prevailing along the Gaza strip resulting from these repeated attacks;

"Notes once again with extremely grave concern that despite the obligation imposed on Egypt by the General Armistice Agreement and a number of Mixed Armistice Commission resolutions, these penetrations and killings of Israel citizens have not been terminated."

In the course of the last week of February, Egyptian military units penetrated about thirty miles into Israel territory, indulging in espionage and murder: on February 23 they broke into Government offices at Rishon LeZion and stole documents, and on February 25 they killed a cyclist near Rehovot. The Armistice Commission found Egypt guilty on all counts. On February 28 an Egyptian military unit delivered an attack across the border on an Israel post. In the hot pursuit that ensued with the arrival of Israel reinforcements, the Egyptians were chased back across the frontier into the Gaza Strip.

The Mixed Armistice Commission describes the position which faced Israel in the Gaza area in the last week of February 1955 in the following manner:

[7] Decision of Emergency Session of Israel-Egyptian Mixed Armistice Commission, 24 Jan. 1955.

"Notes once again with concern the continuous crossings of the Armistice Demarcation line from Egyptian controlled territory into Israel by infiltrators and their illegal actions in Israel;

"Notes further with grave concern the repeated firing from permanent Egyptian military positions on Israel routine patrols operating within Israel territory;

"Notes again with grave concern that despite the obligations imposed by Egypt by the General Armistice Agreement and many Mixed Armistice Commission decisions an end has not yet been put to the aggressive and hostile acts by Egypt against Israel;

"Decides that these aggressive actions constitute a flagrant violation of Article II, para. 2, and Article V, para. 4 of the General Armistice Agreement by Egypt;

"Calls upon the Egyptian authorities to terminate immediately these aggressive actions by Egyptian military positions and the continuous infiltrations into Israel."

Between August 1954 and March 1955 the Mixed Armistice Commission had condemned Egypt forty times. These were certainly no sporadic, unorganized incidents but rather, in the words of the Mixed Armistice Commission, "repeated acts of planned demolition in Israel by well trained, armed and organized groups coming from Egyptian controlled territory."

Israel's defensive action in Sinai and in the Gaza Strip at the end of 1956 eliminated Fedayin bases. Until December 1958 quiet reigned along the frontiers. It was shattered in that month by a Syrian artillery bombardment of Israel border villages, the first of its kind since the invasion by the Syrian Army ten years previously. This bombardment was followed by a similar attack in January 1959 not only as a part of general Syrian aggression along the border, centered particularly around Israel's Demilitarized Zones, but also as an integral part of a policy of intensified war against Israel initiated at the beginning of 1959 by the United Arab Republic when it renewed its interference with the free passage of shipping through Suez.

At the end of 1959, despite the presence of the United Nations Emergency Force stationed along the Egyptian side of the Gaza Strip border, groups of Fedayin raiders again began operations on Israel's territory. It has not yet become clear as to whether these groups were sent on military reconnaissance only or with the intention of renewing murderous attacks against civilians and operating against civilian installations. Nor is it yet clear whether they are the forerunner of more extensive actions in preparation.

Syrian aggresion against Israel's Demilitarized Zones was again renewed at the beginning of 1960, with the infiltration of military units at Khirbet Tawafik. The origin of these Zones is recalled in a note (addenda 12) submitted to the President of the Security Council on 25 February 1960 by Mr. Joseph Tekoah, Acting Head of Israel's Mission to the United Nations:

> "The invading Syrian armies that crossed the international frontiers in 1948 occupied and ravaged certain areas inside Israel. They were still in occupation of these areas when Israel repelled the invading forces of other Arab States, signed Armistice Agreements with them, and was ready to dislodge also the Syrian aggressor. At the urging of the United Nations representative, Israel agreed not to occupy these areas militarily if the Syrian armies withdrew by themselves from Israel's soil. There were to be no other restrictions on Israel in her territories thus regained. In order to ensure that Syria would have no grounds to claim any rights in these areas on the strength of previous occupation by Syrian forces, it was agreed that other Israel areas which had not come under Syrian occupation be added to them, so as to constitute together a Demilitarized Zone on the Israel side of the international boundary. Similarly, a small Demilitarized Zone was established on the Syrian side of the border.*

Under the Israel-Syrian Armistice Agreement, Article V, the Demilitarized Zone in all its parts was created "with a view towards separating the armed forces of the two parties in such manner as to minimize the possibility of friction and incident." Any advance by the armed forces of either party into any part of the Zone would, it was then agreed in Article V, section 5E, constitute a violation: Section 5E makes provision for normal policing activity by Israel as in any other part of Israel sovereign territory. Article V also provides "for the gradual restoration of normal civilian life in the area of the Demilitarized Zone."

In an authoritative interpretation of Article V by the Acting UN Mediator Dr. Ralph Bunche, advanced on 26 June 1949 and accepted by the Israel and Syrian sides before signing the Armistice Agreement, it was made explicitly clear "that the Demilitarized Zone will not be a vacuum or wasteland, and that normal civilian life under normal local civilian administration and policing will be operative in the Zone."

* Report of General Von Horn, Chief of UN Truce Supervision Organization, written in Jerusalem on February 16, 1960 and published as a Security Council document S/4270 of 23 February 1960 (Addenda 13).

Despite the fact that Israel's position in the Demilitarized Zone may be compared to that of Greece in the Dodecanese Islands and of Finland in the Aaland Islands, both demilitarized in 1947—that is, demilitarization did not remove the islands from the scope of full Greek or Finnish control and jurisdiction respectively—the Syrians have from time to time advanced the thesis that the Demilitarized Zone was intended as a no-man's land between the two States. Dr. Bunche's authoritative interpretation explicitly rules out this thesis.

Syrian attempts to renew their policy of military infiltration into the Demilitarized Zone, and hence transform its Israel character into either a no-man's land or Syrian territory, again took place at the beginning of 1960 with the entrenchment of their military units in the abandoned village of Khirbet Tawafiq, southeast of the Sea of Galilee. Attempting to use their military presence there, to interfere with the work of Israeli farmers in the Zone and to extend the area cultivated by Arab farmers, the Syrians precipitated a clash with Israel defense forces which attempted to dislodge them. Although dislodged, they have since returned under cover of a cease-fire arranged by the United Nations authorities.

BLOCKADE OF THE SUEZ CANAL

In defiance of UN Charter and Fundamental Purposes, Egypt announced maritime blockade of Israel in May 1948 and, in violation of General Armistice Agreement with Israel of February 1949 and Constantinople Convention of 1888, has maintained blockade practices against Israel ships and cargoes in the Suez Canal. UN Resolutions condemning practices as well as Egyptian blockade of Israel shipping in Gulf of Aqaba until 1956, consistently ignored by Egyptian Government. Aqaba blockade lifted by Israel defense action in Sinai October 1956—Suez blockade still maintained.

In May 1948, as part of its invasion of that country, Egypt announced its maritime blockade against Israel. With the signing of the Israel-Egyptian General Armistice Agreement on February 24, 1949, containing a categorical injunction (Article 11 (2)) against "any warlike or hostile act by either party," it was taken for granted that this maritime blockade would end. Dr. Ralph Bunche, UN Acting Mediator who helped to bring about the Armistice Agreements, in fact reported to the UN Security Council on July 26, 1949:

"There should be free movement for legitimate shipping and no vestiges of the wartime blockade should be allowed to remain,

> as they are inconsistent with both the letter and spirit of the Armistice Agreements."

The Mixed Armistice Commission, consisting of Egyptian, Israeli and UN representatives, established to implement the Egyptian-Israel Armistice Agreement, decided on August 29, 1949 (S/2047):

> "The Mixed Armistice Commission thinks it has the right to demand that the Egyptian Government shall not interfere with the passage of goods to Israel through the Suez Canal."

Egypt was not only obliged to honor this Agreement made directly with Israel and with the United Nations but her wider undertaking under the Constantinople Convention of 1888, binding her to permit passage through the Canal to ships of all nations, regardless of the relations of these nations with Egypt, required that the international waterway should be insulated from politics. The pertinent clause in the Constantinople Convention states:

> "The Suez Maritime Canal shall always be free and open in time of war as in time of peace, to every vessel of commerce or war, without distinction of flag.
>
> "Consequently, the High Contracting Parties agree not in any way to interfere with the free use of the Canal, in time of war as in time of peace. The Canal shall never be subjected to the exercise of the right of blockade."

In continuous disregard of these UN injunctions and resolutions, and in violation of the 1888 Convention, Egypt, nevertheless, continued her blockade practices in the Canal. An Egyptian Royal Decree of April 3, 1950, contained the following relevant articles:

> "Article 3: It is always permitted to use force, by opening fire when necessary on any ship endeavoring to evade the procedures of search and thus to force it to halt and be searched."
>
> "Article 17: Our Ministers are charged, each in his own sphere, with the implementation of the present decree."

This was followed on July 22, 1950, by new regulations designed by Egypt to strengthen the blockade and to prevent trans-shipments of goods to Israel via a third country. According to these regulations, ships' captains were required to present declarations countersigned by Egyptian consuls in the country of destination, showing that their cargo had actually been discharged and that it was for local consumption. Exactly one month later, Hamid Zaki Bey, Egyptian Minister of State, declared that henceforth Egyptian port authorities would deny drinking water and food to vessels blacklisted for trading with

Israel. As early as the middle of 1950, this "blacklist" already included 88 ships, of which 70 were oil tankers. In September 1950, the Egyptian Government introduced new and increasingly burdensome restrictions such as the requirement of a guarantee by ships' captains, and in particular by captains of oil tankers, that their ships would not ultimately discharge their cargo at an Israel port. Another regulation called for the submission of log books by tankers intending to proceed southward through the Suez Canal. Vessels found to have called at any Israel port were placed on a blacklist and denied stores, fuel and repair facilities in Egyptian ports.

The Egyptian Government Decree of February 6, 1950 formulated a long "list of strategic goods" which might not be shipped to Israel under penalty of confiscation, including such items as petroleum, pharmaceuticals, chemicals, ships, motor cars, money and gold. The obvious aim was to deny Israel use of the Canal for her most important traffic, in particular that of oil. In November 1953, the list was enlarged to include foodstuffs and similar consumer goods.

Israel protested against these measures to the United Nations Security Council in July 1951. During the course of the debate the Representatives of the great maritime powers strongly censured the Egyptian action. Mr. Warren R. Austin, Representative of the United States, condemned Egypt in these words:

> ". . . my Government believes that the imposition of these restrictions, and their maintenance for so long a period after the signing of the Armistice Agreement is a retrogression from what both parties committed themselves to, namely, the establishment of permanent peace in the Palestine area . . . I feel bound also to call attention to the adverse and damaging effect which the Egyptian restrictions have had on the legitimate interests of various maritime nations, including the United States."[8]

Sir Gladwyn Jebb, United Kingdom Representative, in condemning Egypt, stated:

> ". . . there can be no justification for the attempt by Egypt to maintain against Israel restrictions similar to those from which Egypt itself was released two years ago nor can it be said that the Security Council is acting too hastily. Egypt has been given the most ample time and opportunity for lifting these restrictions. During the past two years a number of maritime countries have made almost continual representations to the Egyptian Government through the diplomatic channels, but all these have been of no avail."[9]

[8] Security Council Official Records, 550th Meeting, 16 August 1951. S/PV.552.
[9] Ibid., p. 56.

On September 1, 1951 the United Nations Security Council ordered Egypt "to terminate the restrictions on the passage of international commercial shipping and goods through the Suez Canal wherever bound, and to cease all interference with such shipping." Egyptian claims that a state of war with Israel justified such action were dismissed by the Security Council, which determined that "neither party can reasonably assert that it is actively a belligerent or requires to exercise the right of visit, search or seizure for self-defense," adding that "such practice is an abuse of the exercise of the right of visit, search and seizure."[10]

In direct defiance of this Security Council Resolution, Egypt continued the blockade. The Decree of November 1953, whereby Egypt enlarged the list of so-called contraband goods, stated:

> "Foodstuffs and all other commodities which are likely to strengthen the war potential of the Zionists in Palestine in any way whatsoever."
>
> (Al Misri, November 28, 1953.)

Some of the most flagrant examples of Egyptian blockade practices, after the adoption of the Security Council resolution, included a blacklisting of 70 tankers, the confiscation, on October 31, 1952, of a cargo of meat on the Norwegian vessel 'Rimfrost', the confiscation of building materials and Israel manufactured automobiles from the Greek vessel 'Parnon' at Port Said, the seizure of a cargo of meat and hides from the Italian vessel 'Franca Maria', of clothing and bicycles from the Norwegian ship 'Laritan' and the detention and seizure of the Israel vessel 'Bat Galim', carrying meat, plywood and hides, from Massawa to Haifa, at the entrance of the Suez Canal. The crew of the Israel vessel was imprisoned and maltreated for three months and only released at the intervention of the UN Truce Supervisory Organization, whilst the ship remains in Egyptian hands to this day.

Faced with this Egyptian defiance, the Government of Israel again took its case to the Security Council on February 5, 1954. Again the great maritime powers expressed their protests against Egypt's illegal blockade. The Council's view was summed up by its President, Sir Leslie Munro of New Zealand, who said:

> ". . . any impartial survey of events since the resolution of 1 Sept. 1951 must record that the Egyptian Government has with every appearance of deliberation ignored the injunctions of this

[10] United Nations Document No. S/2322 (1951.)

Council. This course of conduct, persisted in for over two years, has resulted in many ships, which would otherwise have gone on their lawful occasions through the Suez Canal or the Gulf of Aqaba, being deterred from trading with Israel or diverted at great cost over other routes to their destination. No government interested in the preservation of the rule of law in international affairs, and least of all any government dependent for the livelihood of its people on maritime trade, can contemplate this unhappy state of affairs without an earnest desire to bring it to an end."[11]

The draft resolution placed before the Security Council called upon Egypt "to terminate the restriction on the passage of international commercial shipping and goods through the Suez Canal wherever bound and to cease all interference with such shipping . . ."[12] Eight members of the Security Council, including the United States, the United Kingdom, France, Brazil, Denmark, Colombia, New Zealand and Turkey voted for the Resolution, but the Soviet Union vetoed it.

Notwithstanding the expressed stand again taken by the members of the Security Council, the Egyptian Government continued the exercise of its illegal blockade against Israel. The Greek vessel 'Panagia' was detained at Port Said on May 25, 1956, its captain and crew subjected to inhuman harassments for three months, its water supply curtailed and, despite sickness among the sailors, its crew forbidden to go ashore. On July 5, 1956, the Swedish freighter 'Birkaland' was stopped and searched, a member of its crew, found to hold an Israel passport, arrested. In the meantime, the blacklist of foreign ships had reached 120 names, including vessels of British, Scandinavian and American registery.

On October 13, 1956, the United Nations Security Council again resolved that "there should be free and open transit through the Canal without discrimination, overt or covert. This covers both political and technical aspects . . . The operation of the Canal should be insulated from the politics of any country." The unanimous adoption of this Resolution by the Council was in response to the situation created by Egypt's nationalization of the Canal in July 1956. The above quotation is of the major two of six principles unanimously adopted to govern free international navigation in the Canal.

Along with the United Nations and other maritime Governments, the United States expressed its position on the Egyptian blockade practices both in repeated Security Council resolutions and, most

[11] Security Council Official Records, 662nd meeting, 23 March, 1954, S/PV.662.
[12] Ibid.

recently and authoritatively, in a number of statements. Most noteworthy was that of President Eisenhower in a radio-television broadcast to the American people on February 20, 1957:

> ". . . Egypt by accepting the six principles adopted by the Security Council last October in relation to the Suez Canal, bound itself to free and open transit through the Canal without discrimination and to the principle that the operation of the Canal should be insulated from the politics of any country. We should not assume that, if Israel withdraws (from Sinai), Egypt will prevent Israeli shipping from using the Suez Canal or the Gulf of Aqaba. If, unhappily, Egypt does hereafter violate the Armistice Agreement or other international obligations, then this should be dealt with firmly by the society of nations."

During the two years that followed, Egypt desisted from interfering with the passage of ships of other nations carrying Israel cargoes through the Suez Canal. In that period over forty such ships navigated the waterway in both directions, without serious hindrance, after manifests, bills of lading and log books had been examined. On March 9, 1959, the blockade was suddenly reimposed despite the clearcut undertaking by the U.A.R. of April 24, 1957 that "the Government of Egypt are more particularly determined to afford and maintain free and uninterrupted navigation for all nations within the limits of and in accordance with the provisions of the Constantinople Convention of 1888," an undertaking then described by the Secretary-General of the United Nations as "an agreement of an international character." The ship detained on this occasion, the "Capetan Manolis," flying the Liberian flag, was stopped at the entrance to the Canal and her cargo of potash and fruit juices for Ceylon and cement for Malaya was confiscated. Eight days later the vessel "Lealott" of the German Federal Republic was detained and her Israel cargo of cement for Malaya, Hong Kong and the Philippines was confiscated. When the Danish ship, "Inge Toft," en route to the Far East, was detained on May 21, 1959, a wave of protests resulted. On July 3, 1959, replying to such protests addressed to President Eisenhower by twenty-five United States senators against the renewal of Egyptian blockade practices, the Assistant Secretary of State, William B. Macomber, Jr., stated:

> ". . . The United States Government's position with respect to the unrestricted use of the Canal is clear and unequivocal. The United States joined with France and the United Kingdom to sponsor the resolution before the Security Council of September 1, 1951 which called upon Egypt to terminate restrictions on the passage of international commercial shipping and goods through the Canal. This position was reaffirmed by the majority of the

Security Council . . . on March 27, 1954 which called upon Egypt to comply with the 1951 resolution . . . The U.A.R. and all other members of the United Nations are fully conversant with the United States position."[13]

The captain of the "Inge Toft" refused to permit the Egyptian authorities to unload the ship's cargo. Only in February 1960, after an Egyptian refusal to permit the "Inge Toft" to sail northwards, and in view of the deterioration of the vessel, were its Greek owners compelled to permit the unloading and confiscation of the cargo. The captain and crew, who had been subjected to the most trying conditions and who had so courageously withstood Egyptian harassment, then sailed the unloaded vessel back to Haifa.

During the nine months which had elapsed between the seizure and release of the "Inge Toft," Mr. Dag Hammarskjold renewed his efforts to obtain agreement from the Egyptian authorities that ships carrying Israel cargoes should pass freely through the Canal. Following these efforts the Secretary-General informed Israel that he had reason to believe that if Israel would agree to send its export cargoes through Suez in the ownership of the purchaser (that is, F.O.B.) and to import goods intended to pass through the Canal towards her own ports under the ownership of the seller (that is, C.I.F.), the U.A.R. authorities would not obstruct the passage of ships carrying these cargoes.

Israel's reaction to this proposal was later expressed by Mrs. Golda Meir, Minister for Foreign Affairs, in a statement before the Knesset on 22 December 1959:

"Various other parties grasped at this proposal and began to urge us to accept it. We did not regard this method favorably at all. The Government of Israel is not prepared to recognize the right of any one to dictate to it methods of trade that discriminate unfairly against Israel. But those who recommended to the Israel Government to try out this method explained that it would not be long before the U.A.R. authorities would be able to make another step forward and to agree to return to the status quo that existed before the acts of interference that began at the beginning of this year. Everyone who recommended to us the acceptance of this arrangement for the time being emphasized that of course it was contrary to the legal situation, but in view of the intransigeant Egyptian attitude, they believed that we would do better to try it out in practice. We did not succeed in convincing those friendly parties who repeatedly advised us to try out this system, that it had no substance, and that it was only a maneuver of the Cairo authorities designed to mislead friends

[13] Office of Senator Jacob Javits, N. Y., Press Release, July 7, 1959.

of Israel and to create an impression of moderation and of readiness on the part of the U.A.R. to bring about a compromise and reasonable arrangements in regard to passage through the Canal."

It will be recalled that at the time the U.A.R. was negotiating a World Bank loan of 56 million dollars to the Suez Canal Authority for the improvement of the Canal. Whilst these negotiations were going on, the Egyptian dictator undoubtedly wished to create the appearance of such reasonableness and had, without intentions of fulfilment, and shielded by the cloak of "quiet diplomacy," "agreed" to this "compromise" solution.

Israel decided to test the understanding and sent a cargo to Suez in the Greek vessel "Astypalea." On 17 December 1959 the Egyptian authorities detained this ship in Port Said on its way from Haifa to Djibouti. The "Astypalea" was carrying a cargo of 400 tons of cement that had been purchased by an Asmara company. The conditions of dispatch were F.O.B. and the ship was on voyage charter in the name of the purchaser. Prior notification of Israel's intention to send the ship, of the method of dispatch and of the date of departure was given to the UN Secretary-General and to all the friendly parties who advised Israel to adopt this method. The Secretary-General informed the U.A.R. authorities. A complete blackout on all information regarding the ship's movements was imposed to forestall any possible argument, such as had been employed by the Egyptians in the case of the "Inge Toft" to the effect that that ship had been held up because of advance publicity. Between 17 and 22 December 1959 Israel maintained this silence even though knowledge of the detention of the "Astypalea" was in the possession of Israel and of other countries. On 21 December 1959 the World Bank loan was granted to Egypt. Almost three months of the year 1960 have passed and the "Astypalea" is still detained at Port Said.

During her statement of 22 December 1959, when Mrs. Meir broke silence about the "Astypalea," the Israel Foreign Minister stated:

"By this time, however, there is no point in continuing to maintain our silence.... All those who displayed such endless patience with the Egyptian dictator and placed almost boundless confidence in him, must realize by now that he has betrayed them. May we now hope that they have at last been convinced that Nasser must not be trusted, though this remains in doubt. This is not the first time that the Egyptian dictator has broken his promises, even when he gave them to those whe were eager to help him. There are some with whom he has played false time and again.... Only yesterday the Board of Directors of the World Bank approved a loan of 56 million dollars to the Suez Canal Authority. Even if we accept the thesis that the Bank must consider the approval of loans from the economic point of view alone, and need not concern itself with political considerations, there cannot be any doubt that the Bank must not give a reward to a country which violates international law and commits acts of piracy. The granting of this loan for the improvement of the Canal in the face of this conduct on the part of Egypt, its blocking of an international waterway to the shipping of another nation, thus in itself constitutes a political act and Nasser, at any rate, is bound to regard it as an act of encouragement to him to take similar actions in the future."

Until 1957, the U.A.R. attempted to justify its illegal action with legal quibbles. First, Egyptian authorities sought to vindicate their blockade of Israel shipping and cargoes by claiming "belligerent rights." The United Nations, however, clearly stated that under the Egyptian-Israel Armistice Agreement no such rights could be upheld and that, in fact, such claims and the actions they sought to defend were in violation of both the letter and spirit of the Armistice Agreement, the United Nations Charter and the obligation of members to settle disputes by peaceful means.

The second justification, of equal invalidity, has been that under Articles 9 and 10 of the Constantinople Convention Egypt claims the right, as the territorial Power, to take measures for "securing by their own forces the defense of Egypt and the maintenance of public order." By no stretch of the imagination can the hides, chilled beef, cement, fertilizers and similar consumer goods which Egypt prevents from passing through the Canal on Israel vessels or the ships of other countries threaten the security of the U.A.R. Even if such passage were honestly considered by Egypt to constitute such a threat, that would give it no right in law or international contract to refuse free passage. Reliance in such an eventuality on Articles 9 and 10 of the Convention is categorically ruled out by Article 11:

"The measures taken in cases provided by Articles 9 and 10 of the present treaty shall not interfere with the free use of the Canal."

At the same time, Article 4 of the Convention, apart from the ruling of the United Nations Security Council, rejects Egypt's attempted justification for interference with Israel shipping and cargoes as it states explicitly:

"The maritime canal remaining open in time of war as a free passage, even to ships of war of the belligerents, under the terms

> of the present Treaty, the High Contracting Parties agree that no right of war, act of hostility or act having for its purpose to interfere with the free navigation of the Canal shall be committed in the Canal and its ports of access, or within a radius of three nautical miles from those ports, even though the Ottoman Empire should be one of the belligerent Powers."

In the face of mounting world condemnation of its blockade practices, and the transparency of its legal quibble, the U.A.R., since the reimposition of the blockade, has frankly made public its real purpose. The official organ of the Cairo military junta, "Al Gomhuriya" on June 2, 1959, stated:

> "The banning of the passage of Israel ships through the Suez Canal is a vital necessity for the U.A.R. The growth of Israel's economy means the growth of Israel's military power. It destroys the economic blockade which has been imposed by the Arabs ever since 1948."

The Egyptian Government, through Cairo Radio, announced on June 5, 1959:

> "We shall not permit the transit of Israeli goods in the Canal whatever the flag may be. Israel's attempts to break the Arabs' economic blockade will be frustrated."

On June 30, 1959, Colonel Nasser gave an interview to the Egyptian daily, "Al Ahram." During it he stated:

> "Israel has drawn up a well-studied plan . . . attempting to infiltrate into Asia and Africa . . . We must admit that Israel is exerting great efforts to infiltrate into Asia and Africa . . . It is a strange thing that all the Israeli ships which recently attempted to pass through the Canal were carrying goods to African and Asian countries . . . Our stand is that the problem which we are now facing is not a question connected with freedom of navigation . . . Our duty is clear . . . and we shall continue along the road of duty whatever the consequences may be."

On July 2, 1959, as the United Nations Secretary-General, Mr. Hammarskjold, was in Cairo attempting to negotiate the opening of the Canal to Israel shipping, the Government-controlled Radio Cairo announced:

> "The closing of the Suez Canal for Israeli shipping means disrupting Israel's trade with all the countries of Asia and Africa. Israel will not send its goods through the Suez Canal to Asia and Africa . . . Ben Gurion is in a life and death struggle around this issue. We know this and therefore we shall close the Canal and prevent any contact between Israel and these two continents."

The emphasis on legal fiction had thus shifted to a frank admission of the real purpose of the blockade. In line with the general policy of trying to undermine Israel, the blockade, according to the Egyptian view, is one of the most important weapons of an arsenal including general economic boycott, political warfare, etc. It is an integral part of the openly admitted general policy of the U.A.R. as expressed by Colonel Nasser in his speech in Alexandria of July 26, 1959:

> "I am now announcing here in the name of the people of the U.A.R. that we are waiting for a final battle that will bring Israel's defeat. In this battle the dream of the Arabs to exterminate Israel will come true."

Israel again brought the Suez blockade issue to the United Nations on September 24, 1959. The representatives of the majority of States, many of them the Foreign Ministers of their countries, clearly expressed their condemnation of the U.A.R.'s continued defiance and the maintenance of the blockade. Among those who spoke were representatives of the United States, the United Kingdom, Italy, Liberia, Turkey, Bolivia, Iceland, Norway, Belgium, Paraguay, Peru, Sweden, France, the Netherlands, Costa Rica, Australia, Honduras and El Salvador. Following are some typical quotations:

> "The free navigation of the high seas and inter-oceanic canals must be assured, as a fundamental principle of international law, at all times and for all States, including Israel, regardless of the nature of any conflicts which arise in one or another region."
>
> (from the statement of the Foreign Secretary of Uruguay, H. E. Dr. Martinez Montero, at the 805th plenary meeting, Sept. 3, 1959.)

> "In this connection, to mention a somewhat controversial topic, referred to by Mr. Herter, I hope the use of the Suez Canal will form a bond to further, and not a barrier to obstruct, the peaceful trade of all the countries of the area. I have made clear on past occasions the support of Her Majesty's Government in the United Kingdom for the principle of the free passage of ships of all nations through the Suez Canal—a principle which was embodied in the 1888 Convention and which has been adopted by the United Nations as its declared purpose."
>
> (from the statement of the Secretary of State for Foreign Affairs of the United Kingdom, the Rt. Hon. Selwyn Lloyd, at the 798th plenary meeting, Sept. 17, 1959.)

> "We also trust that we can see the freedom of navigation in the Suez Canal re-established according to international law and the

Suez Canal Convention of 1888 which guarantee that the Canal would always be and I quote 'free and open in time of war and in time of peace to every vessel of commerce or of war without distinction of flag. The Canal shall never be subject to the exercise of the right of blockade.' This principle was confirmed by the resolution of the Security Council on 13th October 1956. It is our opinion that the problems of the Middle East will never be solved unless the Arab States themselves show their willingness to solve them together and agree to live together as good neighbors with all the countries in that region."

(from the statement of H. E. Mr. Thor Thors, the Permanent Representative of Iceland to the United Nations, 820th Plenary Meeting, October 5, 1959.)

It should be pointed out that not one non-Arab voice was raised in defence of the U.A.R. position.

Blockade of the Gulf of Eilat (Aqaba)

At the end of 1949, with the permission of the Government of Saudi Arabia, Egypt occupied the islands of Sanafir and Tiran. There, and on the Sinai coast opposite the islands, it established military installations. The purpose was to prevent ships from entering the Gulf of Aqaba destined for the Israel port of Eilat. The implicit capacity of the Gulf and the Port of Eilat to serve as a second short route linking Europe, Africa and Asia was thus held up from 1949 to 1956 by the blockade established by the Government of Egypt.

The blockade was maintained in contravention of the Israel-Egypt and Israel-Jordan Armistice Agreements as Israel's coastline of six miles along the Gulf of Aqaba lies between Jordan on the east and Egypt on the west and is part of the frontiers mutually accepted in these Armistice Agreements. It was also maintained in violation of international law: "The Gulfs and Bays enclosed by the land of more than one littoral state, however narrow their entrance may be, are non-territorial" ("International Law," Vol. 1, p. 508, Oppenheim). This principle was reaffirmed by the International Court of Justice in 1949 in a judgment of general application with respect to the Corfu Channel Case which ruled that vessels of all nations enjoy the rights of free navigation in straits geographically part of a highway used in fact for international navigation, whether or not the straits are entirely or partly within the territorial waters of one or more States. The judgment was:

"It is the opinion of the Court generally recognized and in accordance with international custom that States in time of peace have a right to send their warships through Straits used for international navigation between two parts of the high seas without the previous authority of a coastal state, provided that the passage is innocent. Unless otherwise prescribed in an international convention, there is no right for a coastal state to prohibit such passage through Straits in time of peace."

On January 28, 1950, the Egyptian Government, in a communication to the United States Embassy in Cairo, stated that it had no intention of interfering with peaceful shipping and that "it goes without saying that this passage (through the Straits of Tiran) will remain free as in the past in conformity with international practices and recognized principles of the law of nations."[14]

Called upon by the Security Council to end its blockade in the Suez Canal and the Gulf of Aqaba as illegal and in breach of the 1949 Armistice Agreement, nonetheless the Egyptian Government persisted in defying the Security Council and was able to prevent the free use of this international waterway until November 1956. This was made possible by the narrowness of the lane through the Straits of Tiran, some 500 to 600 yards wide, and only 1,000 yards from the fortified tip of Egypt's Sinai peninsula. The guns which commanded the Straits from Sharm el Sheikh, at the tip of Sinai, and from the islands of Sanafir and Tiran, were only removed when Israel's defense army captured and destroyed the military installations. On the withdrawal of the Israel units from Sinai, a United Nations Emergency Force occupied Sharm el Sheikh to ensure that free passage of shipping, Israel and otherwise, to and from the port of Eilat and to the Jordan port of Aqaba nearby, would be continued. The UN force is currently stationed at this site.

On January 19, 1957 Secretary-General Hammarskjold, in his report to the United Nations General Assembly, stated that neither of the parties to the 1949 Armistice Agreement is entitled to claim belligerent rights, including the application of such rights to the Gulf of Aqaba and the Straits of Tiran. He stated:

"It follows from the findings of the Security Council in 1951 . . . the parties to the Armistice Agreement, may be considered as not entitled to claim any belligerent rights . . . and will not assert any belligerent rights (including of course such rights in the Gulf of Aqaba and the Straits of Tiran)."[15]

[14] "The Gulf of Aqaba: An International Waterway," by Paul A. Porter. (Public Affairs Press, Washington, D. C.). Page 3.

[15] Ibid.

On January 15, 1957, but four days earlier, the Secretary-General, in a note to the General Assembly, had underscored that the Gulf of Aqaba and the Straits of Tiran constitute international waterways.

On February 11, 1957, in the course of its negotiations for the withdrawal of Israeli troops from Sharm el Sheikh, the United States embodied its views on the international character of the Gulf of Aqaba and the Straits of Tiran in a memorandum made public on February 17. The memorandum stated:

> "The United States believes that the Gulf comprehends international waters and that no nation has the right to prevent free and innocent passage in the Gulf and through the Straits giving access thereto. We have in mind not only commercial usage, but the passage of pilgrims on religious missions, which should be fully respected.
>
> "The United States recalls that on 28 January 1950 the Egyptian Ministry of Foreign Affairs informed the United States that the Egyptian occupation of the two islands of Tiran and Sanafir at the entrance of the Gulf of Aqaba was only to protect the islands themselves against possible damage or violation, and that 'this occupation being in no way conceived in a spirit of obstructing in any way innocent passage through the strech of water separating these two islands from the Egyptian coast of Sinai, it follows that this passage, the only practicable one, will remain free as in the past, in conformity with international practices and recognized principles of the law of nations.'
>
> "In the absence of some overriding decision to the contrary, as by the International Court of Justice, the United States, on behalf of vessels of United States registry, is prepared to exercise the right of free and innocent passage and to join with others to secure general recognition of this right."[16]

The international character of the Gulf of Aqaba was confirmed in the Convention of the Territorial Sea and the Contiguous Zone, adopted by an International Conference at Geneva on April 29, 1958. Article 14 of the Convention confirms the right of innocent passage and Article 15 expressly states:

> "The coastal state must not hamper innocent passage through the territorial sea."
>
> Article 16 provides:
>
> "There shall be no suspension of the innocent passage of foreign ships through straits which are used for international navigation between one part of the high seas and another part of the high seas or the territorial sea of a foreign port."

[16] Ibid., pages 4-85.

Since the lifting of the Egyptian blockade of the Gulf of Aqaba by the Israel army, Eilat has begun to prosper as a port of exit and entry for Israel's trade with Africa and the Far East, and the overland route between Eilat and the Mediterranean provides an invaluable link between the Red and Mediterranean Seas. Not only does shipping bound for the Israel port of Eilat proceed unhampered on its rightful way, but also international shipping bound for Aqaba, the Jordanian port, is similarly unrestricted.

THE ARAB ECONOMIC BOYCOTT

Economic boycott, as an Arab weapon of warfare against the Jews, dates back to the period of the British Mandate. It was introduced by the Palestine Arab Higher Committee, headed by Haj Amin Husseini, the pro-Axis Mufti of Jerusalem, in an attempt to strangle, subdue and destroy the growing Jewish community in Palestine. It reached its height at the end of the thirties with the attempt to deny the use of Haifa as a port to the Jews which resulted in their building at the time the port of the all-Jewish city of Tel Aviv which broke the blockade. As the Governments of the adjoining Arab countries became more and more influenced by Nazi Germany and Fascist Italy, the boycott against the Jewish community of Palestine, more and more identified with the democracies, became part and parcel of their "solidarity" with the Mufti.

Thus the Arab economic boycott of Israel and Israel products, which has been growing in intensity since the signing of the Armistice Agreements in 1949, is the re-adaptation of a weapon which failed before 1948 and its re-employment, in violation of the Armistice Agreements, on a more efficiently organized plane. Its objective has been defined by Abdul Kerim Ayidi, Supervisor of the General Boycott Office, at a conference of representatives of Branch Offices held in 1957:

> "A continuation of the boycott would lead to Israel's being wiped out, as it is already having a serious effect on its political, industrial and economic life."[17]

Even more explicit was the statement by the Beirut (Lebanon) Boycott Offices

> "People tend to believe that the foremost aim of the boycott is to prevent Israel goods from reaching the Arab countries and

[17] Business International, May 17, 1957.

Arab goods from reaching Israel. Actually this is only a secondary aim. The Boycott Office has set itself two objectives: a) to sabotage the industrialization of Israel; b) to obstruct the export of Israel commodities."[18]

A more recent definition of the boycott was given in "Al-Bulis," official periodical of the Egyptian Police Force published in Cairo, which stated on August 30, 1959:

"How to throw Israel into the sea? Israel cannot be destroyed by force and therefore must be destroyed economically. If the Arabs can prevent Israel's economic expansion, they would hasten its end... Israel can achieve economic independence by marketing its products in the neighboring countries of Asia and Africa. But Israel is exposed to an economic boycott by the Arabs which blocks her way to the Arab markets. Closing of the Suez Canal to ships carrying goods will now prevent her from reaching the markets of Asia and Africa."

The majority of Arab countries have passed legislation forbidding their nationals to maintain any contacts or commercial relations with Israel. Penalties of up to 10 years imprisonment with hard labor and maximum fines of $14,000 may be imposed for infringement of these laws.

The Arab States have maintained a complete suspension of all postal, telephone and telegraph facilities between themselves and Israel, and have interrupted all communications by sea, air, road and rail.

The Boycott Offices put pressure, amounting to blackmail and threats of coercion, upon business concerns operating both in the Arab countries and Israel, to force the closure of their Israel branches. Foreign Governments have not been immune to this pressure, designed to deter them from conducting negotiations or concluding trade agreements with Israel.

An example of this pressure upon business concerns in foreign countries has been the recent withdrawal from business operations in Israel of the Renault automobile enterprise of France. The Cairo daily "Al-Massa" of November 25, 1959, commented:

"The U.A.R. has won a great victory this month in its economic warfare against Israel with the closing down of the Renault plant and the final liquidation of its business in Israel. This event proves that the Arab economic boycott, which aims at the prevention of the use of any Israeli products, has succeeded.

[18] Le Commerce du Levant, Beirut, August, 1954.

We are facing now a new campaign which we will start next winter; namely, the occupation of Israel's citrus markets in Europe."

In answer to a question about the Renault company's withdrawal from Israel by deputy M. Charret on October 30, 1959, the French Foreign Minister, M. Maurice Couve de Murville, stated before the National Assembly:

"The boycott initiated by the countries of the Arab League, with several of which the French Government has not maintained diplomatic relations since the end of 1956, is manifestly contrary to international law. This boycott constitutes, however, through the force of circumstances, a factor which could, without doubt, be of a nature to exert influence on the evaluation which a firm investigating the markets can apply regarding the respective importance of these markets."

The General Boycott Office has its headquarters at Damascus in Syria. Branch Offices are administered by the Ministry of Commerce in each of the Arab States, which prepares and disseminates "blacklists" to Arab commercial and consular representatives abroad.

Imports to and exports from Arab States require special licenses, certificates of origin and destination, and endorsement by Arab diplomatic personnel in the countries involved. The Arab States send lists of their exports to the General Office so that Arab Missions overseas, including in the United States, may check chances of trans-shipment in violation of boycott regulations.

Boycott extends to Jews of all countries

The boycott is not confined to Israel and Israel citizens. For several years it has reached over to Jews and Jewish firms, even though they may have no connection, private or commercial, with Israel.

Saudi Arabia takes the lead in discrimination against Jews and any concern employing them in any capacity. The U.S. Department of Commerce reported.[19]

"Saudi Arabia intends to boycott all Jewish or Jewish-directed firms trading with that country, according to information received by the Bureau of Foreign Commerce. This new policy greatly extends the provisions of the existing boycott against firms having branches, assembly plants, or general agents in Israel, as well as firms having shares in Israeli companies. Implementation of a new policy normally will be accomplished by Saudi Arabian Consulates

[19] "Foreign Commerce Weekly," March 5, 1956.

who are responsible for registration of commercial invoices and certificates of origin."

"Fortune" magazine reported, in its August, 1957, issue: "Businessmen throughtout the world were in receipt a month ago of a strange questionnaire. Dated Cairo, Egypt, the questionnaire pressed them for information on whether their firms were guilty of having Jewish ownership or participation."

The Public Affairs Institute of Washington reported: "The boycott was applied to foreign firms having Jewish directors."[20]

The London Chamber of Commerce was asked to certify that British firms wishing to trade with Arab countries were not Jewish.[21]

Saudi Arabia, Jordan, Iraq, Syria and Yemen refuse entry or transit visas to Jews regardless of nationality.[22] American citizens and nationals of other countries visiting Israel are not allowed to enter Arab countries directly thence. They are refused visas to Arab States, if there is evidence that they have visited or intend to visit Israel. The U.S. Department of State informs passport applicants that Jews among them will be denied the right to visit many Arab countries. The American Export Line informs passengers on ships touching at Arab ports that those of Jewish faith or with "Jewish" names will be denied travel facilities in Arab countries, available to other passengers. American and other international airlines flying to the Middle East indicate in their time-tables that Jewish passengers will not be allowed to deplane at Arab airports en route.[23]

Since 1945 Saudi Arabia has refused to permit American Jews to be stationed as members of the U.S. armed forces at Dhahran Air Base. The agreement, signed in 1951 and renewed in 1957, requires the U.S. Mission to submit "a detailed list of the names and identities" of its members and employees so that it will not include "individuals objectionable to the Saudi Arabian Government."[24]

Under boycott prescriptions, vessels may not call at Israel and Arab ports on the same run. American Export Lines, for example, must run a second Middle East service, expensive and time-consuming,

[20] *Regional Development for Regional Peace,* Public Affairs Institute, Washington, D.C., 1958, p. 276.

[21] "New York Times," October 15, 1957.

[22] The Jordan Government Tourist Brochure expressly states: "Nationals of all countries (except Israel and *members of the Jewish faith*) are permitted entry into Jordan provided they hold a valid passport with an entry visa."

[23] See p. 12 of "A Report on the Arab Boycott against Americans" (Presidents of Major American Jewish Organizations) Feb. 1958.

[24] U.S. Treaties and Other International Acts Series, No. 2290.

to Haifa and Tel Aviv. More than 120 ships of foreign register have been blacklisted for sailing to Israel. These include a number of American ships.[25] Arab League States threaten to confiscate goods consigned to Israel aboard foreign vessels touching at Arab ports.

The Boycott in the Air

Planes making use of Israel facilities are forbidden to over-fly Arab territories, to seek flight information, or obtain rescue services from Arab sources.[26] Saudi Arabia vows to shoot down any aircraft flying over its territory bound to or from Israel. These restrictions and menaces are in violation of the Convention on International Civil Aviation and of the International Air Service Transit Agreement.[27]

The Oil Boycott

Major American and British oil companies yielded to the boycott at the start. The flow of oil from Iraq to the Haifa refinery was halted in 1948 and has not been resumed. A projected Haifa terminal for Tapline, conveying oil from Saudi Arabia to the Mediterranean, was abandoned under Arab pressure in favor of terminal points in Syria and Lebanon. For many years the Haifa refinery, formerly owned and operated jointly by the Royal Dutch-Shell Group and the Iraq Petroleum Company, worked at only half or one-third capacity. It has now been handed over to Israel ownership and management. The oil companies will not send their tankers to Israel through the Suez Canal, which means burdensome freight charges for Israel; they ceased to market in Israel and to prospect for oil there.

Boycott Hampers Work of International Organization

The boycott hampers the work of international bodies and stultifies the purposes for which they were founded. Members of the Arab League will not attend their meetings if Israel is present. An Arab League resolution lays down the conditions:[28]

> "If these conferences were held in any Arab State, no visas or permission for entry should be granted Israel's representatives to attend. Participation in regional conferences organized on the

25 "Fortune," August, 1957.
26 "New York Times," October 15, 1957.
27 United Nations Treaty Series, Vol. 15, 1948, pp. 296-360, No. 102. Ibid., vol. 84, 1951, pp. 391-399, no. 252.
28 No. 354 of May 19, 1951.

initiative of one country or by an international organization could not be attended if Israel were also invited."

The policy of non-cooperation with Israel wrecked the U.S.-sponsored Johnston plan for the multilateral development of Middle East water resources, although the technical experts of all the countries concerned were in agreement on its feasibility.

In an article in the "New York Times" magazine of October 19, 1958, Ambassador Eric Johnston himself stated:

> "After two years of discussion, technical experts of Israel, Jordan, Lebanon and Syria agreed upon every important detail of a unified Jordan plan. But in October 1955 it was rejected for political reasons by the Arab League. Syria objected to the project because it would benefit Israel as well as the Arab countries. Three years have passed and no agreement has yet been reached on developing the Jordan. Every year a billion cubic meters of precious water still roll down the ancient stream, wasted in the Dead Sea."

Air safety is jeopardized by Arab refusal to join a single flight information center for the Middle East. Operations of the UN Locust Control Commission are impeded. There is no effective Regional Council of the World Health Organization or other Specialized Agencies of the United Nations in the Middle East.

In October, 1951, the Arab League decided not to participate in any UN regional conferences under the auspices of the UN if Israel were also to attend. A few examples of how this decision has been implemented will suffice:

> "The Arab States will boycott the Izmir Fair (in Turkey) because of Israel's participation." "El Ahram," 29 June 1955
>
> "The Arab Governments refuse to attend the Sessions of the World Health Organization if Israel is represented there... They will leave the WHO if its director insists on his present stand." NEAB, 7 July 1955
>
> "The Arab States will not participate at the Congress of Military Surgeons, to be held in Turkey, because of Israel's intended participation." "El Ahram," 14 July 1955

In a report to the United Nations Economic and Social Council (Commission on Narcotic Drugs, 15th Session) by the Middle East Narcotics Survey Mission, one of the most harmful effects of the Arab boycott of Israel is underscored:

> "There is a large scale traffic flowing from the north through Jordan, over the Israeli border, across the Negev desert, then

over the Israel-Egyptian border and on to a market in Egypt. The smugglers' efforts along this route are well organized and coordinated but there is no cooperation whatever between enforcement forces. The reason for this situation is a well known political one and thus beyond the scope of the Mission to comment on—it can only point out that while the situation exists the smugglers have all the advantages. The attention of the Mission was drawn to a pact being negotiated between Turkey and Iran which is designed to strengthen and improve liaison arrangements at the enforcement level between these two countries. This is a pattern which could be followed with advantage by other countries."[29]

The Civilized World Fights the Boycott

There is ample evidence that, firmly resisted, the boycott fails. West Germany pays restitution year after year to Israel for property seized or destroyed by the Nazis, and between 1953 and 1955 the dollar value of German exports to boycotting Arab countries rose from $95 m. to $124 m.

In 1956 the Central Organization for Foreign Economic Relations at the Hague advised members of the Netherlands Branch of the International Chamber of Commerce not to supply Arab importers with information about Jews employed in Netherlands export houses. Dr. W. Drees, Netherlands Foreign Minister, emphasized that his Government would resist all Arab boycott attempts infringing Dutch interests. He pointed out that the boycott is "illegal and conflicts with the Armistice Agreements."[30]

Individual business concerns throughout the world have likewise withstood Arab pressure. A British firm reacted typically in the following terms:

"We vigorously contest the right of any overseas body or Government to dictate to us where we shall or shall not market our goods. Our business is that of selling our products anywhere in the world, and in this we are actuated by commercial considerations alone, politics play no part whatever in our sales policy. We do, in fact, maintain strict neutrality in all our dealings with various countries and that, in our opinion, is eminently more desirable than taking sides on issues completely unconnected with the affairs of England. The only edicts we obey are those of our own Government and provided they do not impose restrictions

[29] United Nations Economic and Social Council, Commission on Narcotic Drugs, 15th Session, Middle East Narcotics Survey Mission, Report, Communicated by the Secretary-General, Doc. E/CN.7/382, November 16, 1959, p. 11.

[30] "Netherlands News Bulletin," September 21, 1957.

on the export of our goods to any particular destination, we regard ourselves as free to sell wherever there is demand."[31]

Failure of the Boycott

Nearly eleven years of Arab economic warfare have not checked Israel's economic growth and the possibility of its inflicting vital injury is slight. It has been a weapon of spite rather than a serious danger to Israel development. In some respects it has even served to stimulate Israel's economic progress by encouraging a larger agricultural output and the discovery of new export markets.

On the other hand, Jordan's refusal to accept free port facilities at Haifa, offered by Israel, costs that country an advantageous outlet to the Mediterranean and Western Europe, and retards the development of its mineral resources. Iraq oil revenues are impressively contracted by closure of the pipe-line to Haifa.

Before the boycott, Jewish Palestine took 90% of Jordan's exports, and was also a profitable market for agricultural produce from Syria, Lebanon and Iraq. In turn Jewish industry in Palestine found a natural emporium in neighboring Middle East countries. Resumption of this complementary and mutually remunerative exchange would provide a welcome economic impetus to the region.

The boycott aggravates and perpetuates tension, and flouts the principles of economic international intercourse. It sins against the Armistice Agreements of 1949, which called upon all signatories to cease hostile acts. It thwarts the main purpose of the Agreements, which is the conclusion of permanent peace in the Middle East. It disregards the United Nations Charter, which requires members to settle differences by peaceful means. It endangers the peace of the world, because boycott and blockade are instruments of warfare.

[31] "A Report on the Arab Boycott Against Americans," p. 23. (Pub. by Presidents of Major American Jewish Organizations), Feb. 1958.

CHAPTER XI

The Middle East Refugees

1. The Arab War against Israel created two refugee problems. Arab political and military leaders organized a mass flight of Arabs from Israel territory in order to facilitate military operations. Some 587,000 Arabs abandoned their homes in consequence. Simultaneously, Arab persecution of Jewish minorities caused an exodus from Moslem countries of nearly half a million Jewish refugees who were forced to abandon property valued at hundreds of millions of dollars.

2. Jewish refugees were absorbed as citizens of Israel and found work and homes. The Arab States oppose any solution of their refugee problem, which they regard as a political weapon for use against Israel, careless of the human suffering involved. For them the Arab refugees are a potential fifth column for the destruction of Israel.

3. The abundance of cultivable land in the Arab States, the prevailing shortage of manpower, the availability of $200 million in funds approved by the UN for resettlement projects, the readiness of Israel to pay compensation for abandoned property, the fact that the Arab refugees speak the language, practise the religion, and share the culture of the citizens of their host countries—all these factors render the Arab refugee problem permanently soluble.

4. World public opinion now takes the view that the refugees should be re-settled in Arab countries through large-scale economic development schemes.

Causes of the Problem

The U.N. partition resolution provided for an Arab minority of just over 400,000 in the new State of Israel. When the Armistice Agreements were signed, only 160,000 Arabs were resident in that territory. By now their number exceeds 220,000.

Before 1947, roughly 747,000 Arabs had lived in what is now Israel. It is reckoned that, during the hostilities of 1947-48, 587,000 of them left and were classified as refugees.

The Arab war against Israel produced a second refugee problem —Jews, who left the Old City of Jerusalem and the Arab lands of the Middle East and North Africa, as a direct or indirect consequence of the War. Between 1949 and 1958, 476,000 such Jewish refugees were absorbed by Israel.

Iraq	125,000
Yemen	50,000
Arab-held Old City of Jerusalem	1,700
Egypt	60,000
Other Arab League countries	240,000

The refugee problem sprang from the Arab invasion of Israel. The Arab League Governments have raised no finger to rehabilitate their refugee brethren, victims of their own belligerent propaganda. Israel has shouldered the entire responsibility for the immigration and resettlement of Jewish refugees, giving them full rights of citizenship. Only Jordan of all the Arab States, has allowed citizenship to Palestine Arabs.

At no time had the Jews envisaged a mass Arab departure. For months before the proclamation of the State, Jewish leaders urged the Arabs to abandon civil strife. On December 7, 1947, Haganah distributed leaflets in Arab villages calling on the inhabitants "to keep the peace and remain calm."[1] Histadrut, the Jewish trade union movement, made similar appeals to Arab workers. The Arab leaders would not listen to these voices of goodwill.

From the very start, the State of Israel held out a hand of friendship to the Arabs. The Proclamation of Independence declared:

> "Even amidst the violent attacks launched against us for months past, we call upon the sons of the Arab people dwelling in Israel to keep the peace and to play their part in building the State on the basis of full and equal citizenship and due representation in all its institutions, provisional and permanent."

[1] Joseph B. Schecht, *The Arab Refugee Problem*, p. 2.

The counsel went unheard, but Arab overweening confidence in victory quickly veered to panic as Israel betrayed no sign of collapse.

The Arab exodus had begun much earlier, immediately following the UN partition resolution of November 29, 1947, when 30,000 members of rich Arab families in Jerusalem, Haifa and Jaffa left for the neighboring Arab countries. In no sense could these be said to be refugees: they were in fact actuated by fear of what the policy of Arab extremists might bring about and had ample time and opportunity to transfer their assets to new homes in Arab lands.

The second phase set in early in 1948, when thousands of Arabs moved from the coastal area to the hills. The Jews were at this time on the defensive. The chief spur of Arab flight was propaganda of the Palestine Arab Higher Committee, insisting that the terrain be cleared for campaigning Arab armies. During this period 6,000 Arabs left Tiberias (April 18), 60,000 left Haifa (April 22) and 70,000 left Jaffa (April 25-29).

In other words, over 200,000 had left their homes in Palestine before the State of Israel was established, and at a time when it was the Arabs who were on the offensive.

After the renewal of fighting on July 9, when the Arabs turned down Count Bernadotte's proposals for extending the first cease-fire, about 250,000 other Arabs left Israel, and when the second truce broke down, there was a third trek of Arabs from northern Galilee into Lebanon and from the south into Gaza.

Arab Responsibility for the Refugee Problem

It is established fact that defiance of the 1947 UN partition resolution by the Palestine Arabs and the neighboring Arab States created the problem.

The Palestine Arabs' use of force in opposing the decisions of international tribunals had gone on for some three decades. The League of Nations in 1922 had made the Mandatory Government responsible for the establishment of the Jewish National Home through "Jewish immigration" and "close settlement of Jews on the land." Throughout the whole period of the mandatory regime, the Jewish community in Palestine spared no effort in the quest for friendly cooperation with its Arab fellow-citizens. The Arab answer was intransigence and attacks on Jewish villages and on individual Jews: Arab violence in 1920, 1921 and 1929, and in 1936-1939, punctuated a period in which hundreds of Jews were murdered and much Jewish property, acquired over long years of arduous labor, was pillaged. On the morrow of the adoption of the partition resolution by the United Nations, the Palestine Arabs, with the assistance of the neighboring Arab States, started a chain of belligerency which developed into the Arab invasion of Israel and an aggressive war to defeat the peaceful carrying-out of the compromise determined by the United Nations.

Speaking before the Special Session of the UN General Assembly on March 16, 1948, the Lebanese representative, Mr. Camille Chamoun, referred to "the violent opposition of the overwhelming majority of the people of Palestine" to that compromise. A month later, Mr. Jamal al Husseini, on behalf of the Palestine Arab Higher Committee, declared in the Security Council: "The representative of the Jewish Agency told us yesterday that the Arabs had begun the fight... As a matter of fact, we do not deny this fact... We told the whole world that we are going to fight."[2]

In this predicament, the United Nations Palestine Commission, charged to implement the partition resolution, had, as will be recalled, to report to the Council in February and April 1948 that "powerful Arab interests both inside and outside Palestine are defying the resolution of the General Assembly and are engaged in a deliberate effort to alter by force the settlement envisaged therein."[3]

The Arab exodus took place at the behest of Arab commanders and political leaders who persuaded the Arab populace that evacuation to neighboring countries would be brief and that they would soon return behind victorious Arab armies and share the spoils.

Responsibility for the consequences of the defiant and internationally rebellious hostilities launched against Israel, of which the refugee problem is only one, rests, therefore, fairly and squarely upon the Arabs, and, in certain moments of candor, they have recognized that themselves:

> "The Arabs would not submit to a truce... They rather preferred to leave their homes in the town (Haifa), which they did."[4]
> "Winter is approaching and the refugees are without shelter. Responsibility for them and for failing to settle the affair rests on these Arab States which look idly on."[5]

[2] Security Council Official Records, Third Year, No. 58, 283rd meeting, 16 April 1948, p. 19.

[3] (A/AC.21/9, February 16, 1948, U.N. Document).

[4] Jamal Bey Husseini, spokesman for the Palestine Arab Higher Committee, Security Council Official Records, Third Year, No. 62, 287th meeting, 23 April 1948, p. 14.

[5] King Abdullah of Jordan, My Memoirs Completed.

"The fact that there are these refugees is the direct consequence of the action of the Arab States in opposing partition and the Jewish State. The Arab States agreed upon this policy unanimously, and they must share in the solution of the problem."[6]

"The Secretary-General of the Arab League, Assam Pasha, assured the Arab peoples that the occupation of Palestine and of Tel Aviv would be as simple as a military promenade... He pointed out that they were already on the frontiers and that all the millions the Jews had spent on land and economic development would be easy booty, for it would be a simple matter to throw the Jews into the Mediterranean... Brotherly advice was given to the Arabs of Palestine to leave their land, homes and property and to stay temporarily in neighboring, fraternal States, lest the guns of the invading Arab armies mow them down."[7]

"Who brought the Palestinians to Lebanon as refugees, suffering now from the malign attitude of newspapers and communal leaders, who have neither honor nor conscience? Who brought them over in dire straits and penniless, after they lost their honor? The Arab States, and Lebanon amongst them, did it."[8]

An American observer:

"The Arab exodus, initially at least, was encouraged by many Arab leaders such as Haj Amin el Husseini, the exiled pro-Nazi Mufti of Jerusalem, and by the Arab Higher Committee for Palestine... They viewed the first waves of Arab setbacks as merely transitory. Let the Palestine Arabs flee into neighboring countries. It would serve to arouse the other Arab peoples to greater effort, and when the Arab invasion struck, the Palestinians could return to their homes and be compensated with the property of Jews driven into the sea."[9]

The refugees themselves:

"All of a sudden, the people of Jaffa began to evacuate their town, abandoning it in the middle of a fight, even before its climax... I now see that we fought only half-heartedly... Our many quarrels kept us too busy. We left the country of our own free will believing we were going on a short visit, a trip, and soon we would return as if nothing had happened and as if there had never been a war."[10]

"The Arabs were confused by promises and deluded by their leaders... Iraq's Prime Minister had thundered:

[6] Emil Ghoury, Secretary, Palestine Arab Higher Committee, "Daily Telegraph," Beirut, September 6, 1948.

[7] Habib Issa. Editor, "Al Hoda," Lebanese newspaper in New York, June 8, 1951.

[8] Kul-Shay, Moslem weekly, Beirut, August 19, 1951.

[9] Kenneth W. Bilby, "New Star in the Near East," Doubleday, New York, 1950, pp. 30-31.

[10] Mahmoud Seif ed-Din Irani, "With the People", Amman, Jordan, 1956.

'We shall smash the country with our guns, and destroy and obliterate every place the Jews seek shelter in. The Arabs should conduct their wives and children to safer areas until the fighting has died down.'[11]

"The Arab Governments told us:

'Get out so that we can get in!' So we got out, but they did not get in.[12]

The British confirm it:

"The situation in Haifa remains unchanged. Every effort is being made by the Jews to persuade the Arab populace to stay and carry on with their normal lives, to get their shops and businesses open, and to be assured that their lives and interests will be safe."[13]

"Of the 62,000 Arabs, who formerly lived in Haifa, not more than 5,000 or 6,000 remained. Various factors influenced their decision to seek safety in flight. There is but little doubt that the most potent of the factors were the announcements made over the air by the Higher Arab Executive, urging the Arabs to quit... It was clearly intimated that those Arabs who remained in Haifa and accepted Jewish protection would be regarded as renegades."[14]
"It must not be forgotten that the Arab Higher Committee encouraged the refugees' flight from their homes in Jaffa, Haifa and Jerusalem."[15]

"The Arab civilians panicked and fled ignominiously. Villages were frequently abandoned even before they were threatened by the progress of war."[16]

All this further underscores the responsibility of Arab leaders for inciting mass flight from Palestine. To hasten it they circulated stories of atrocities and fabricated reports of massacres.

Nevertheless, 160,000 Arabs, many of them Christians with much to fear from Moslem majorities, held their ground, discounted the intimidation and stayed unharmed in their villages. Through repatriation and natural increase, their number has since risen to over 220,000. They are citizens of Israel, enjoying equal rights and opportunity with

[11] Nimer Al-Hawari, ex-Commander, Palestine Arab Youth Organization, "The Secret Behind the Disaster".

[12] "A-Diffa", Jordan, September 6, 1954.

[13] British District Police, Haifa, report to Police Headquarters, Jerusalem, April 26, 1948. (This was among the documents in the police files which came into the possession of Haganah.)

[14] "Economist," London, October 2, 1948.

[15] Near East Arabic Broadcasting Station from Cyprus, April 3, 1949.

[16] General Glubb Pasha, Commander of the Arab Legion, "Daily Mail", London, August 12, 1948.

Jews. Their condition is infinitely better than that of fellow Arabs anywhere in the Middle East.

This is reflected in an article entitled "Exodus Revisited," by Leon Uris, the celebrated author, published in "Look" Magazine, November 24, 1959. Under the picture of a tractor driven by an Arab citizen, the author writes: "One in ten Israelis is an Arab. This one, driving a tractor through busy streets, knows he belongs to the best-housed, best-educated and freest Arab community in the Middle East."

It is also reflected in a statement by Dr. Robert G. Storey, Dean, School of Law, Southern Methodist University, who is also Chairman of the United States Board of Foreign Scholarships and member of the President's Commission on Civil Rights, which was published in the "Dallas News" on January 5, 1959:

> "Israel can teach the nations of the world a lesson on how to conduct their relations with their minority groups. I was greatly impressed with the manner in which the Arab population had been made an integral part of the general community life."

CONSEQUENCES OF THE PROBLEM AND ITS SOLUTIONS

The Arab refugees have become a principal weapon of propaganda for the Arab States against Israel. Those States have made no effort to settle and rehabilitate the refugees in their midst, but instead have used them as a source of friction and harassment. Only Jordan, which annexed a large part of Mandated Palestine, a part that, under the UN partition resolution, was to be within the borders of a Palestine Arab State, has granted them citizenship. That this is what the Arab leaders want is clear from their refusal to cooperate either among themselves or with the United Nations in taking adequate measures for relief and for settlement of the problem.

Arabs Oppose Return

At the beginning of their attack on Israel, when they anticipated quick success, the Arabs made no demand for the return of the refugees. In fact, they vehemently opposed it. "It will serve as a first step towards Arab recognition of the State of Israel and partition," was the view of Emil Ghouri, Secretary, Palestine Arab Higher Committee.[17]

[17] In "Daily Telegraph," Beirut, August 6, 1948.

The United Nations General Assembly resolution 194 (111) of December 11, 1948 observed that "the refugees wishing to return to their homes and *live at peace with their neighbors* should be permitted to do so at the *earliest practicable date* . . ." The same resolution also called upon "the Governments and authorities concerned... to seek agreement by negotiations conducted with a view to the *final settlement* of all questions outstanding between them." Individual repatriation was hence subject to three clauses: (1) the practicability clause, (2) the "live at peace" clause and (3) it is clear from the terms of the resolution that the settlement of the refugee problem constitutes part of the "final settlement of all questions outstanding between the Arab States and Israel."

The Arab States voted unanimously against the General Assembly resolution of December 11, 1948, calling for peace negotiations between them and Israel and asserting that "refugees wishing to return to their homes and live in peace with their neighbors should be permitted to do so at the earliest possible date." Arab insistence on the implementation of this part of the resolution, *in isolation from its other and integral parts* (the "live in peace" clause and the "final settlement" clause) was hardly consistent with logic, justice or legality.

The United Nations Palestine Conciliation Commission, which was created by the December 11, 1948 resolution, rejected the singling out of the refugee paragraph by the Arab States from the resolution as a whole. The Commission declared that "the Palestine problem must be considered in its entirety."[18] It further made it clear that "in considering the Palestine problem in its entirety the Commission was following guidance given to it by the General Assembly (in the December 11, 1948, resolution). The Assembly resolution under which the Commission operated and under which the delegations of the Arab States and Israel were operating with it—emphasized the general character of the Palestine problem."[19]

At the time the December 11, 1948, resolution was adopted by the Assembly, the United Nations hoped that peace would be quickly restored in the Middle East. Even so, the Assembly by the expression "as soon as practicable" admitted by inference that at the time of adoption of the resolution the return of the refugees to Israel was considered as impracticable. This clause is therefore legally a "suspensive condition." Subsequent developments resulting primarily

[18] Report of the U.N. Palestine Conciliation Commission. U. N. Doc. No. 181 A/1985 pp. 3-4.
[19] Ibid. P. 76.

from the Arabs' refusal to come to any terms of settlement with Israel made the idea of large-scale repatriation so impracticable that, save for its use as a propaganda weapon by the Arab States, it has been more or less abandoned by the world community and the integration of the refugees into their countries of residence has been stressed in its place.

Chronologically, it was not until the spring of 1949 that the Arab leaders reviewed their stand and began to demand re-admission. But they still shunned peace negotiations, the essential prerequisite to any substantial Arab return to Israel. The position of the Arab States was clearly represented by Mohammed Salah e-Din, the Egyptian Minister for Foreign Affairs, when he stated on October 11, 1949, in an article in the leading Egyptian daily, "Al-Misri":

> "In demanding the restoration of the refugees to Palestine, the Arabs intend that they shall return as the masters of the homeland, not as slaves. More explicitly they intend to annihilate the State of Israel."

REFUGEE ATTITUDE TOWARDS ISRAEL

There has been ample testimony from the Arab side that the refugees, if allowed back would not think of living "at peace with their neighbors." Arab leaders have always looked upon that return as a means of destroying the Jewish state from the inside, on a par with economic boycott, maritime blockade, border warfare, infiltration by terrorists and preparation for invasion. It is an open secret that their repatriation demand is part and parcel of Arab political warfare and propaganda against Israel:

> "The Arab refugees will not be returned to Palestine except by war, which will preface their return. Palestine Arabs only demand arms, mobilization and training. The remainder they will do themselves."[20]

The refugees are regarded as a fifth column: "let us therefore try to make them our fifth column for the day of revenge and reckoning." "El Sayad," Beirut, Lebanon, April 6, 1950.

In furtherance of this aim of subversion, military training centers for Palestine Arabs were set up in Egypt, Jordan and Syria.

[20] "Falastin," Jordan daily, Jan. 28, 1956.

ARABS BALK AT FINAL SETTLEMENT

The Arabs have persistently refused to negotiate any final settlement of outstanding issues between themselves and Israel, recommended by the General Assembly resolution of December 11, 1948, of which the context and spirit imply that negotiations of that character were regarded as a condition precedent to any large-scale re-admission of refugees.

Arab antagonism to any practical solution of the refugee problem is summed up by Mr. Ralph Galloway, former UNRWA representative in Jordan, addressing a group of American Congressmen in Amman in 1952:

> "It has been the growing recognition of the international community that the solution to the refugee problem must be found through programs of rehabilitation and large-scale development projects which will make the refugees self-supporting members of their host countries, as well as contribute to the economic development of those countries. It has been increasingly recognized that such plans for a solution are constantly hampered and frustrated by political objection by the Arab countries which are not interested in any realistic solution to the problem but in keeping it as an open sore, as an affront against the United Nations, and a weapon against Israel."

Arab spokesmen frankly confess the reason for their obstructionism. The Foreign Minister of Iraq told a party of American newspaper correspondents:

> "The refugee problem is being used by Egypt as a political football. Iraq alone is capable of absorbing all the Arab refugees, amounting to more than a million souls. In Iraq there are wide expanses of uncultivated agricultural lands waiting to be tilled. It is within Iraq's capacity to absorb more than 5,000,000 people."[21]

"L'Orient," Beirut, said in April, 1957:

> "The responsibility of the Arab Governments is very great. For eight years they have been applying to the refugees an abstract and inhuman policy; under the pretext of cultivating in the refugees the longing for their homes in Palestine, and for the purpose of maintaining a menacing population on the frontiers of Israel, they have systematically rejected all attempts at organization and employment for the refugees."

[23] "Rose el Yussef," Cairo, April 8, 1957.

The Arab States have not only thwarted any progress towards a final settlement of the problem. They have assiduously blocked all proposals for easing the situation of the refugees.

In reaction to the "Report on Arab Refugees to the United Nations"[22] by Mr. Dag Hammarskjold, Secretary-General, dated June 15, 1959, the Beirut daily, "El Hayat," wrote on June 24, 1959:

> "The flood of comments which followed the United Nations Secretary-General's report again demonstrated the negative Arab attitude which tends to criticize, accuse and threaten.
>
> "Firstly, it should be noted *that the Arabs today are the last people interested in the return of the refugees or in trying to render them justice. The Arab States use the suffering of the refugees as a weapon in their struggle.* But this struggle has not yet taken place and it does not look as though the Arab States were getting ready now to wage it in the near future. Eleven years have already passed, the refugees are still scattered and time has begun to leave its mark on them. The old generation is disappearing and the new generation, foreign to its motherland, has arisen.
>
> "During all these years, *the Arab Governments have not lifted a finger* in order to bring justice to the refugees. If this situation will continue for another ten years, the refugees will disappear, memory of them will be forgotten and the new generation will assimilate in its new country.
>
> "We have already stated that the Arab States need a positive policy towards the Palestine problem. The whole Arab mentality requires a basic change in this matter. Ever since the Arabs opened their struggle against the Jews of Palestine in the second decade of this century they have followed a purely negative policy, centering round the word "NO," without reference to any practical steps. We constantly demand what we would like to see and never think about what we could obtain in reality. Accordingly, we have achieved nothing ever since we rejected the British White Paper of 1939. The events in Palestine have developed contrary to our aspirations but we still did not act according to our abilities and were not satisfied with achieving the possible. As a result, we have now been living for over a third of a century in wild imaginations, in senseless and impractical hopes, and enjoy a mirage of lies and ignorance... We repeat and reiterate our warning that we are on the brink of a new disaster... We still continue to delude ourselves, refuse to change our mentality and

[22] This report constituted the basis for discussion at the meeting of the Special Political Committee of the UN General Assembly in November, 1959, when the question of the Palestine Arab refugees and the future of UNRWA came under review.

> face facts... When shall we have a practical policy based on Arab, regional and international facts?
>
> "The world laughs at the Arabs when Palestine is being discussed, and tomorrow history will say: *"In the Palestine problem the Arabs were the victims of their ignorance, blindness and arrogance."*

The U.S. Ambassador James J. Wadsworth, addressing the United Nations Ad Hoc Committee, as far back as November 16, 1955,[23] emphasized the need for "programs which will make refugees self-supporting... We are sure that in making that start our Arab friends understand that what will benefit the Arab refugees will benefit the Arab countries themselves.

> "The plan for the development of the Jordan Valley, which has been the subject of intensive and fruitful negotiations between Ambassador Eric Johnston and the interested countries in the area, will bring 120,000 acres of new land into cultivation in the Kingdom of Jordan alone... providing many thousands of Arab refugees and their other fellow-Arabs with new and self-respecting means of livelihood. It will also create new jobs, new facilities, new industries... It is a start for a new and better Arab world.
>
> "However, the United States alone, the contributors of funds to UNRWA alone, the United Nations itself, cannot bring this about unless the leaders of these Arab nations will let us help them help themselves. We believe that they can, to the benefit of their countries, view the refugees as an important asset, not, as is often implied here in debate, an unwanted liability. Upon these leaders' shoulders rests the choice, we believe, between progress to greatness and prosperity and the narrow clinging to the status quo which benefits no one but those who profit from misery and chaos."

This view is again upheld by the Lebanese daily "El Hayat" which on June 25, 1959, stated:

> "The Beirut press announced yesterday that the Lebanese Foreign Ministry has instructed its representative at the United Nations to inform Mr. Hammarskjold that the Government of *Lebanon disagrees* with his report *on the resettlement of the refugees in the Arab world.*
>
> "Undoubtedly, similar notifications will be sent to the Secretary-General by the other Arab States.
>
> *"Isn't this a perfect example of our hypocrisy? Is there any other Arab country in which these refugees have been more fully absorbed than in the Lebanon?*

23 80/PV.15

"Of the 120,000 refugees who entered the Lebanon in 1948 no more than 15,000 have been left in camps. If we remember that the natural increase during these years has reached a similar figure of 15,000 we must accept the conclusion that all of the 120,000 refugees have been absorbed in the Lebanon and have become an integral part of its population, society and economic life.

"Nevertheless, we refuse to 'resettle' the refugees—in our typical Arab way, that of the ostrich!

"It would have been understandable had the Arab States rejected the resettlement of the refugees in the Arab world and had kept them instead on the borders of Palestine and organized them, both politically and militarily, for a new war. But the refusal to resettle them in the way we go about it is worse than Mr. Hammarskjold's proposals and even Israel's hopes...

"It is only regrettable that the refugees themselves have been prepared to lend themselves to this policy of blindness. They have not succeeded in organizing themselves properly in order to prevent the Arab States from leaving the right track. History will determine that our brothers the refugees are in a very large measure responsible for their tragedy because of their primitive emotions and hopeless enthusiasm.

"*Everybody in the Arab States, among the refugees, and all over the world knows that we the Arabs, in our present position and on the basis of our present policy, will not do a thing for the refugees.* Nevertheless, we 'reject' resettlement and accuse any foreigner who dares mention the word 'resettlement' of treason, imperialism and intrigue; even if he only wants to help us or the refugees.

"The time has come for us to rid ourselves of this hysteria of verbal bravery and empty dreams at our expense and at that of the refugees. The time has come for the Arab States to forgo their ambition to compete for the support of the mobs in a contest of words about Palestine and to move from a policy of 'crocodile tears' to one of plans, means and aims."

PROPOSALS FOR SOLVING THE PROBLEM

It is more than obvious that the solution lies in programs of rehabilitation and large-scale development projects to make the refugees self-supporting citizens of their host countries. As far back as 1950, the General Assembly envisaged "the re-integration of the refugees into the economic life of the Near East . . . in preparation for the time when international assistance is no longer available."

In 1957 the Director of the United Nations Relief and Works Administration (UNRWA) reported:

"Officials of the host Governments, with but two exceptions . . . oppose large-scale resettlement projects . . . The two large-scale projects which have been under study for some time . . . are considered technically possible but . . . they are held up because of political and other factors beyond our control."[24]

The U.S. Delegation to the United Nations underlined this report by stating:

"the host Government did not respect their obligations . . . these projects have proved feasible and technically sound, but unfortunately, no agreement on them has materialized."[25]

The U.S. Congress has repeatedly urged realistic solutions. A Survey Mission to the Middle East, sent by the House Committee on Foreign Affairs, reported: "It is essential that they (the Arab States) realize that the refugees are people who are with them to stay. Furthermore, it is not sound for the United Nations to continue camp operations in the face of continuous hostility and harassment . . . frequently on the part of the host Governments."[26]

A few quotations from a speech to the Special Political Committee of the United Nations on 10 November, 1958, by George McGregor Harrison, the United States Delegate, revealed the gravity of the situation:

"Today there are more refugees who need help than there were in the past. Despite UNRWA's efforts which have been great and, considering the obstacles, successful.

"Clearly something must be done. Over the past ten years the world has given some $200,000,000 to help the refugees, the United States having contributed two-thirds of this amount. The world generally, including the contributors, have a legitimate interest in a solution. Over the past two years the United States has urged that advance planning be undertaken looking toward the expiration of UNRWA's mandate in 1960.

"In our view it is not good enough consciously to perpetuate for over a decade the dependent status of nearly a million refugees. Finally, those Governments whose contributions year after year have made it possible for UNRWA to sustain the refugees are becoming increasingly critical of the dole that they are called upon to perpetuate.

"The continuation of UNRWA beyond its present mandate, is not, in the eyes of the United States, the proper way to handle the refugee problem . . . Some better system must be found that

24 Report A/SPC/9 February 11, 1957.
25 A/SPC/SR. 26, February 21, 1957.
26 February 24, 1954.

will greatly accelerate the rate at which refugees are made self-supporting."[27]

The Senate Committee on Foreign Relations Report on the Mutual Security Act, 1955, stated: "A permanent solution of the Arab refugee problem can only be found through rehabilitation and resettlement and the Committee has repeatedly expressed its deep concern over the lack of progress in this direction."[28]

In a document entitled "Proposals for the Continuation of United Nations Assistance to Palestine Refugees," submitted by Mr. Dag Hammarskjold, Secretary-General, the practical possibilities of fully integrating the refugees is summed up in these words:

"Given the present economic situation in the area, we can, in general terms, state that the re-integration of the refugees through normal economic processes into productive life will, for the immediate future, at least, require capital imports sufficient to render possible an increase in national income and capital formation preferably more than proportional, but at least proportional, to the increase in population. From an economic viewpoint, such capital imports would represent sound investment in an area with great potentialities and great needs for a more diversified production. In the long run, with increasing revenues from oil in some parts of the region, the emphasis would switch from capital imports to investment of surpluses in the areas where re-integration takes place . . . Viewed from an economic angle, the re-integration of the Palestine refugees into productive life, although it must be considered as a fairly long process, is perfectly within reach . . . Viewed from the perspective of what has been said, the unemployed population represented by the Palestinian refugees should be regarded not as a liability but, more justly, as an asset for the future; it is a reservoir of manpower which in the desirable general economic development will assist in the creation of higher standards for the whole population of the area."[29]

RETURN NO LONGER FEASIBLE

Proposals to restore the refugees *en bloc* to the homes that they abandoned in Israel have been increasingly frowned upon by the international community. Arab spokesmen, too, admit that the demand for such restoration does not stem from consideration for the welfare of the refugees themselves.

27 United States Delegation to the Gen. Assembly, Press Release No. 3068, 10 Nov. 1958.
28 Senate Report No. 383, 84th Congress, 1st Session, May 27, 1955.
29 Document A/4121/Corr.1 29, June 1959, pp. 3 and 4.

Yet it has been a focal point of Arab propaganda against Israel for more than ten years. The Arabs, as has been shown, regard it as an instrument in their war to obliterate Israel.

We again recall the words of Major Salah Salem, a member of the Egyptian Cabinet at the time, who in 1955 declared:

> "Egypt will strive to erase the shame of the Palestine War, even if Israel should fulfil the United Nations resolution; it will not sign a peace treaty with her even if Israel should consist only of Tel Aviv."

OPPORTUNITIES FOR SOLUTION

The United Nations and its agencies have made effort after effort to set in train programs directed towards a final solution of the Arab refugee problem.

As far back as 1949, George McGhee, Assistant Secretary of State for Near Eastern Affairs, stated: "The problem could be solved economically rather than politically."[30]

The Palestine Conciliation Commission, established by the United Nations in 1949, dispatched an Economic Survey Mission to the Middle East, headed by Gordon R. Clapp, to estimate the capacity of the Arab States to absorb refugees in development projects. The Mission came up against overwhelming Arab resistance. Its reports highlighted the merits of integrating the refugees in the Arab countries of the Middle East, and recommended the substitution, in a extensive public works program, of constructive activity for philanthropic relief.[31]

Overborne, however, by the Arab States, the Mission's final report switched to a recommendation of four small-scale pilot projects in Jordan and Lebanon (December 22, 1949).[32]

In December 1949, the General Assembly established the United Nations Relief and Works Agency for Palestine Refugees in the Near East (UNRWA). The design was that the Agency should provide not only relief but constructive works programs to furnish employment. But it has encountered the sustained opposition of the Arab States in its attempts to carry out this essential part of its function.

30 Joseph B. Schechtman, The Arab Refugee Problem, Philosophical Library, New York, 1952, p. 43.

31 United Nations Conciliation Commission for Palestine, Final Report of the UN Economic Survey for the Middle East, Pts. I and II (A/AC.25/6), 28 December 1949, Appendix IA, pp. 14-30.

32 "Ibid."

In June 1951, John D. Blandford, Jr., then Director of UNRWA, put forward a plan to resettle between 150,000 and 200,000 refugees in Arab countries within the space of a year.[33]

The Arab refugees are the only group of refugees in the world in continuous receipt of international charity. From the beginning they have been wards of the United Nations. Never has there been a problem of the kind with so many factors making a solution possible. They are living in countries with which they share a common culture, faith and language. Ample international funds are to hand to finance a resettlement which will not cost the host countries a farthing and will be all to their monetary and economic gain. Israel has pledged compensation for abandoned lands, and the U.S. Government in 1955 announced its readiness to lend Israel the money for payment of that compensation. Great tracts of empty land, fit for settlement and development, await the plough in Arab countries. Notably in Iraq and Syria there is a shortage of manpower.

Dr. Elfan Rees, Adviser on Refugees to the World Council of Churches, reported as follows to the Geneva Conference on Refugees on May 27, 1957:

> "I have often wondered how long the patience of the contributing governments will last, to contribute to the perpetuation of a refugee problem which, they know very well, was capable of solution . . . I dare to suggest that there is also a debt owed to the refugees by the Arab States themselves—the debt that men of the same language, the same faith, the same social organization, should at any time in history feel due from them to their fellows in distress. The debt which in simple terms would involve regarding these people as human beings and not as political footballs."

Returning to this question, in his booklet "We Strangers and Afraid," Dr. Elfan Rees stated again in 1959:

> "The debt of the Arab States is one of fellowship and compassion—a debt that has been paid by many nations in this era of refugees to homeless men of the same race and faith. It is high time that a people so famous for their hospitality to the wanderer should see the tragedy of hopelessness and idleness and become more aware of human needs and less concerned with the political advantages—which are not what they were—of having a refugee problem."[34]

[33] Schechtman, op. cit., p. 58.
[34] "We Strangers and Afraid" by Elfan Rees, Pub. by The Carnegie Endowment for International Peace, p. 57.

OTHER REFUGEE PROBLEMS SOLVED

Since 1914, 40 million people have been displaced as a result of war and social disorder. In no single instance has repatriation solved the problem.

After the First World War, nearly two million persons were involved in population transfers in Turkey, Greece, and Bulgaria. During the Second, 900,000 persons belonging to 52 ethnic groups were transferred or exchanged in Central and Eastern Europe. After it, 12 million Germans were moved into Germany from Czechoslovakia, Poland, Hungary and Yugoslavia. More than 2,500,000 persons were exchanged between Poland and Russia.

When India was partitioned in 1947 into the new States of India and Pakistan, no fewer than 13 million people, Moslems from India and Hindus from Pakistan, moved across the new borders. All preferred the security and affinity with their own kith and kin, with their own people sharing the same community of culture, religion, language and history, to the continued role of an oppressed or suspect minority in an alien environment. None disputed the obvious implications inherent in their self-uprootment that a homogeneous life with their own people is more desirable than dangerous dependence for existence itself, materially and culturally, upon the good will, level of political education and consciousness and tolerance of the majority. This two-way exchange of population, for this voluntary movement was in fact just this, dwarfed in its dimensions a similar movement caused by the partition of Mandatory Palestine.

JEWISH REFUGEES FROM ARAB COUNTRIES

Although that partition was not accomplished peacefully, as envisaged by the United Nations General Assembly resolution of November 29, 1947, but, instead, in violation of that resolution by Arab invasion of the territory and by war, the movement of Arab refugees from Israel's territory and of Jewish refugees from the Arab countries is a striking parallel.

The waves of anti-Jewish terrorism in consequence of the Arab invasion of Palestine and the successful defense of the State of Israel by its founders swept away the last barriers to Jewish disfranchisement and elimination in Iraq and Syria and contributed to the exodus of Jews from Yemen, Libya, Egypt, Morocco and Tunisia as well. These waves of terrorism could have been expected in countries where Jews had lived as second-class citizens and had been subject to repeated outbreaks of religious fanaticism and persecution. From 1933 onwards their situation had further deteriorated as a result of the penetration of Axis propaganda and influence particularly in the army and among students in countries such as Iraq and Syria where the ex-Mufti of Jerusalem had been permitted to inflame the population with anti-Jewish sentiments. The pogroms against Jews when the pro-Axis Government came to power in Iraq at the beginning of World War II heralded the inevitable consequences for the Iraqi Jewish community of the invasion of Palestine in 1948 by the Iraqi army. The anti-Jewish measures in Syria during and after the invasion of Palestine by units of the Syrian army in 1948 were a continuation of decades of anti-Semitism in that country. Whilst Israel's open door provided a solution to the problems of Jewish communities in the Arab countries, the immigration of Jews from those countries to Israel was speeded by their plight in the Arab States. The War of 1948 triggered the flight of 476,000 Jewish refugees from the Arab countries (a process which under varying degrees of restriction continues). It was, however, but a major episode in a long and bitter story of persecution, second-class citizenship and dependence.[35]

Whilst the State of Israel welcomed the Jewish refugees from the countries of the Middle East and North Africa as kith and kin, bearing the main economic and social burden of their absorption, the Arab States, which by their invasion of Palestine in the first place had created the Arab refugee problem, refused to absorb the victims of their aggressive war. They chose instead to perpetuate their distress as refugees as a political weapon against Israel in callous indifference to their fate.

In none of the instances mentioned, which involve numbers many times greater than does the Palestine case, has repatriation been deemed a way of lightening refugee distress. The overwhelming majority of these displaced persons have, by their own efforts and with official help, made new homes for themselves within their new lands.

Not only has Israel borne the major cost of the absorption of 476,000 Jewish refugees from Arab lands. Despite the continued war of the Arab States against her by economic boycott, maritime blockade, infiltration, border assault and incessant incitement at home with the

[35] A detailed picture of the plight of "Jews in Moslem Lands" may be obtained from the booklet of that title published by the Institute of Jewish Affairs, World Jewish Congress, in June 1959.

undisguised objective of launching a war of annihilation against her. Israel has during this entire period made frequent unilateral gestures of a pacific nature unprecedented in such international relations. Without bearing guilt for the Arab war of aggression or responsibility for the Arab and Jewish refugee problems it produced, Israel accepted back 48,500 Arab refugees under a compassionate policy of re-uniting divided families, and resettled them during the same period when she had to bear the grievous burden of finding permanent employment and housing for the hundreds of thousands of Jewish refugees from the Arab countries. The United Nations Palestine Conciliation Commission has paid warm tribute to Israel's action in releasing bank accounts and deposits to the value of 11 and one-half million dollars in favor of Arab refugees. While the Arab States maintained their ruthless economic warfare against Israel, this transfer of hard currency to hostile territory finds no parallel in the relations of nations. To this day German assets, frozen during World War II, still remain in American banks awaiting their liquidation as part of a permanent peace settlement.

Time and again Israel has renewed her offers to pay compensation for abandoned lands as an important contribution to Arab refugee resettlement. As such a burden of full and immediate payment of all the sums involved would have faced Israel's population with a commitment beyond its powers, the Government of Israel responded formally and affirmatively to a proposal made in 1955 by the Secretary of State of the United States to provide Israel with an international loan to discharge such an undertaking. This unilateral offer still maintained, without any accompanying offer by the Arab States to compensate Jewish refugees forced to abandon their properties in the Arab States in consequence of the same Arab war of aggression, is again without international precedent. It should be recalled that, when the over 120,000 Jews from Iraq were forced to leave that country between 1949 and 1951, their abandoned assets, liquid and immovable, were auctioned and the proceeds expropriated by the Iraqi Government of the time.

In short, without responsibility for the Arab-Israel war and the twin refugee problems that war produced—of Palestine Arabs who voluntarily left Israel's territory and Jews forced by hostility and persecution to leave the Arab states of the Middle East and North Africa—Israel and the Jewish people have borne the full cost of resettlement of the Jewish refugees and the State of Israel has offered and continues to offer compensation to aid in the resettlement of displaced Arabs. As a further contribution towards a peaceful settlement of problems in the area and dissipation of its tensions, Israel's Ambassador, Mr. Abba Eban, in a statement before the Special Political Committee of the General Assembly of the United Nations on November 17, 1958, renewed Israel's offer of compensation even without demanding as a condition that it be part of an overall peace settlement between Israel and the Arab States. This offer, again unique and without parallel, was made in these words:

> "The basic solution of the refugee problem lies in the integration of the refugees in the countries where they have been for the past decade, and where they live among their own kinsmen. There is no precedent for a country which has been the victim of aggression voluntarily offering compensation to other victims of the aggression. Nevertheless, we have made this undertaking. *If such a solution by integration were actually carried out and if the international assistance offered (the loan suggested by Mr. Dulles) in 1955, were available, Israel would be prepared to pay compensation, even before the achievement of a final peace settlement, or the solution of other outstanding problems.* We believe that even if a peace settlement is beyond our reach, there would be independent advantage, both moral and political, in a separate solution of the refugee problem. For this reason we are now disposed to envisage a settlement of our compensation undertaking in advance of a settlement of other outstanding questions, provided only that substantive solution of the refugee problem were actually implemented. In fixing the level of compensation owed by Israel it would be necessary to take into account the claim of Israel citizens who have a right to compensation for property left behind in Arab lands. In the context of such a solution by integration in Arab lands, and the fulfillment of Israel's compensation undertaking—we do not exclude an extension of the uniting of families scheme under which many former Arab residents have already come back to Israel territory . . . The international community longs to see this problem solved, not perpetuated. Generous assistance is available to the Arab Governments if they will open their homes, lands and hearts to their own kinsmen. Israel, as I have explained, would make its due contribution to a serious international enterprise designed to integrate the refugees into the life of the region. The advantages which Arab Governments now appear to find in the artificial maintenance of this problem are barren and unrewarding if, indeed, they exist at all. May 1960 be a turning point—away from the sterile obstruction of the past decade towards a solution in which realism, honor and compassion join hands for the sake of regional welfare and international peace."

CHAPTER XII

The Arab Community in Israel

Israel's Arab community now numbers over 220,000. Government policy aims at its complete economic and political integration with the Jewish community, in fullest cultural and religious freedom. Israeli Arabs enjoy all the rights and privileges of citizenship. With Government and other public encouragement they have made great forward strides in health, education and economy. Wartime restrictions in sensitive border areas, required by the continuing state of war proclaimed by Israel's Arab neighbors, are being progressively eased and removed.

ISRAEL'S POLICY regarding her Arab community, now numbering over 221,500 (about 152,000 Moslems, 47,500 Christians, and 21,500 Druzes), pursues twin objectives: first, the raising of economic, social, cultural and health standards to the general Jewish level; second, a still present need for internal security dictated by the refusal of the Arab States to make peace. Israeli Arabs are a constant target of propaganda warfare from Cairo, aimed at stirring up subversive elements. They are urged to be disloyal to Israel and warned that "collaboration" will brand them as traitors.

For all that, the great percentage, on the whole, are loyal and law-abiding and have earned a steady relaxation of security measures, even if Israel's Arab neighbors forgo nothing of their aggressive acts and designs.

At the outset of independence, the Government of Israel carried out a complete registration of all citizens. Adults, Jews and Arabs, were given identity cards. Some border areas are under minimal restrictions of movement as a precaution against infiltration. The majority of the Arab population live in such border areas, but the restrictions are territorial, not communal, and resident Jews are affected by them equally with Arabs. Some 36,000 Arabs inhabit the vicinity of the Jordan frontier between Kfar Saba and Megiddo, where Israel's over-all width from the Mediterranean to the border is barely ten miles. Thousands more live close to the frontiers with Syria and Lebanon in the north. Twenty thousand nomads live in the Negev, within easy reach of the Egyptian-held Gaza Strip and southern Jordan. For the many more thousands of Arabs, in Nazareth, Western Galilee and Judea, reasonably distant from the borders, there is no Military Government and movement is utterly free.

In conspicuous contrast with Arab discrimination against Jews in Egypt, Iraq and other Arab countries, the Arabs in Israel possess the same economic, social and political rights as the Jews. They have complete freedom of speech, assembly and worship. Arabic is a recognized language for official purposes, including its use by Arab members of the Knesset (Parliament). Education in Arab schools is conducted in Arabic. From the age of 18, all Arabs have the right to vote by secret ballot in local and parliamentary elections. At 21, they may be candidates for local councils and the Knesset. In the general election of June 1955, 91% of the Arab population voted for candidates of their own choice, a higher percentage than among the total electorate. There are four Arab political parties and eight Arab members of the Knesset. Unlike their sisters in most Arab countries, all Arab women in Israel enjoy the franchise. A large number of Arabs are members of the Civil Service, including teachers, physicians, social workers, police officers, administrators and judges. Arabs are presently exempt from compulsory military service, for self-evident security reasons, pending an improvement in Israel-Arab affairs which might dispel certain obvious hesitations both of Israel's Ministry of Defense and, naturally, of Israel's Arabs themselves. But Druzes, of whom there are, as said, 21,500 in Israel, are not exempt and, as it is, not a few Arabs volunteer to serve.

Arab economic life has been transformed since the establishment of the State. The feudal system of land tenure has virtually disappeared, and 80% of Arab farmers own their land. The rest work as laborers for the same Trade Union wages as Jewish members of the Histadrut, which has 15,000 full-fledged Arab members, and organizes widespread vocational training for them.

The main endeavor of the Government to better Arab standards of living has, understandably, been in agriculture. Arab farmers receive seed, fertilizers, livestock and insecticides from Government sources. They profit from the expansion of water supply, irrigation, electricity and road facilities. The Government has assigned agricultural instructors and made special loans to Arab farmers, to enable them to institute more modern and intensive methods of agriculture and to engage cooperatively in ancillary industries.

Large demand for agricultural products, resulting from Jewish immigration, has led to a considerably larger volume and value of Arab farm produce. Since 1948, that value has multiplied six times. Irrigation means that two and more crops are now harvested where previously only one grew.

The circumstances of Arab unskilled laborers have been improved almost as spectacularly: their daily wages are more than twice what they were worth in 1948.

Under the Compulsory Education Act of 1949, all Arab children from the ages of 5 to 14 are guaranteed free elementary education as are all Jewish children. As a result, nearly 80 per cent of the Arab school age population is receiving education, compared with 45 per cent in Egypt and 35 per cent in Iraq. As in education, tremendous progress is being made in health. Malaria and trachoma, formerly endemic in Palestine, have been wiped out, whilst tuberculosis has been brought under control by inoculation and X-ray treatment. Arab health centers, providing pre and post natal care for mothers and children and general medical services, have undoubtedly contributed to the high standard of life prevalent amongst Israel's Arab citizens, whilst the introduction of electricity and pure running water to more and more Arab villages has made life much easier.

This progress was reflected in a speech by Associate Justice William O. Douglas of the United States Supreme Court, delivered on June 20, 1959, in New York City. He stated:

> "The Arab stands before the law on the same footing as the Jew, and that is a fact, for there are some 200,000 Arabs, I believe, in Israel, and there is no discrimination. They are in the Histadrut and some of them are even in the Parliament. They have their schools and they enjoy the same work opportunities.
>
> "That is a wonderfully inspiring, important symbol to keep alive. That is the greatness of America, too—room for the minority, room for every minority, room for every point of view, room for everybody to stand up and talk.

> "And that is one of the great glories of the political system in Israel: it makes room for all groups—racial, religious and political."

Professor Rushbrook Williams, a former Fellow of All Souls College, Oxford, and for many years a member of the "London Times" editorial staff, in his book, "The State of Israel," had this to say about the position of Israel's Arab citizens:

> "The Jewish majority seems determined to accord to all minorities within the country the kind of treatment which it would have liked (and which it so rarely received) in all the epochs and in all the lands in which it experienced the trials of existence under the rule of a majority differing from itself. There is a continual and active demand for what can only be called specially-favored treatment for the Arabs."[1]

[1] Rushbrook Williams, "The State of Israel," New York, Macmillan Co., 1957, pp. 198-199.

CHAPTER XIII

Jerusalem – Capital of Israel

Jerusalem has occupied a unique position in the life of the Jewish people for over 3,000 years. It was the political capital of their country for centuries of national independence and the spiritual center of their religion and tradition in nearly 2,000 years of dispersion. The resurrection of the State of Israel in 1948 made inevitable the restoration of Jerusalem as its capital.

THE UNITED NATIONS PROPOSAL in 1947 to internationalize Jerusalem was shelved when the Arab States disowned it and launched war against Israel. It is now obsolete. The Arab beleaguerment of Jerusalem in 1948, while the world stood helplessly by, united the New City and its inhabitants forever to the body of Israel.

It will be recalled that the UN partition resolution, of November 29, 1947, recommended the establishment of independent Jewish and Arab States in Palestine and a separate international status for Jerusalem and its environs under UN authority. All three areas were to be associated in an economic union. The plan was conceived as a coherent whole, on the assumption that it would be generally accepted and implemented by all parties in all its parts.

The Jews accepted the resolution with certain reservations. The Arabs rejected it *in toto,* and specifically opposed an international regime for Jerusalem on the ground that it would infringe the right of self-determination.

Their position was formulated by Faris el-Khouri, later Prime Minister of Syria, at the Security Council on April 1, 1948:

"The Arabs certainly do not agree to the establishment of a permanent trusteeship regarding the City of Jerusalem, for the reason that though there are Holy Places located in Jerusalem, I feel that the people of Jerusalem are not holy. They are not to be given special consideration and special privileges, nor are they to be deprived of the rights of democracy and self-determination, which are enjoyed by all the people of the other democratic countries. The shrines and Holy Places may be protected and given all the necessary safeguards, but the people should be left their freedom and liberty in order to determine their fate and their future administration in the way in which they wish, just as any democratic country would confer privileges and rights upon its population."[1]

At the second Special Session of the General Assembly, on May 14, 1948, other Arab representatives emphasized their dislike of a separate status for Jerusalem. Mahmoud Fawzi, now Foreign Minister of Egypt, declared that internationalization of Jerusalem:

"is most clearly a violation of the right to self-determination which the people of Jerusalem should enjoy as well as any other people in the world. Moreover, it is recognized that the people of Palestine, including those of Jerusalem, are quite ripe for independence . . . There is no reason why just because they live in Jerusalem they should be accorded special treatment different from that accorded to the other people of Palestine."[2]

The Iraq representative, Awni Khalidi, claimed that internationalization was contrary to the United Nations Charter:

"The Charter does not justify the United Nations or, for that matter, one Delegation, to tear away a city from a country and put it under trusteeship. It does not entitle the United Nations to super-impose a set-up against the very wishes of the population."[3]

The Jordanian position has been consistent throughout the years. In 1952 Said el Mufti, Deputy Premier and Minister of the Interior, who had formerly served as Prime Minister, declared:

"We do not recognize internationalization and we shall never change our position even if all the Arab States oppose it."[4]

On January 21, 1957, Abdullah el-Zureikat, Chargé d'Affaires of the Jordanian Embassy in Baghdad, declared:

[1] Verbatim Record, p. 71.
[2] A/P.V. 135, May 14, 1948.
[3] Ibid.
[4] Falastin, September 28, 1952.

PRINCIPAL HOLY PLACES

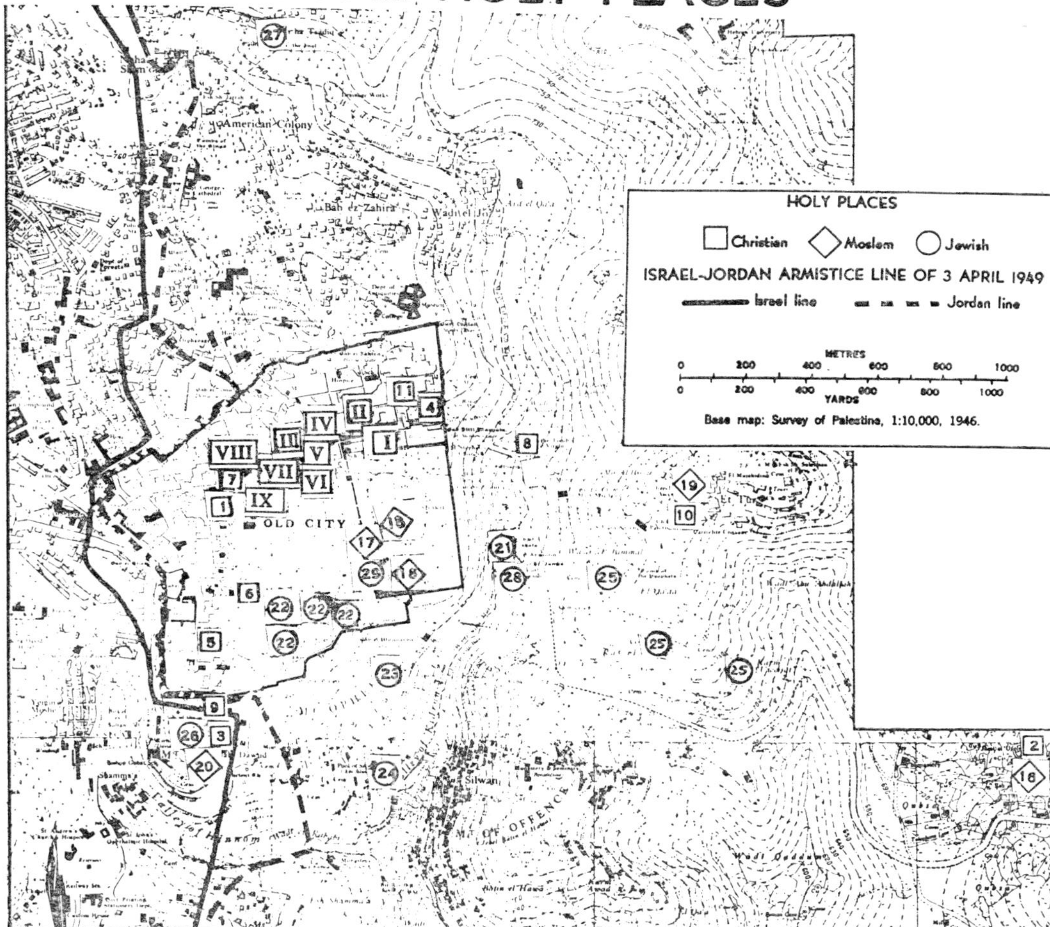

LIST OF HOLY PLACES

CHRISTIAN

1. Basilica of the Holy Sepulchre*
2. Bethany
3. Cenacle
4. Church of St. Anne
5. Church of St. James the Great
6. Church of St. Mark
7. Deir al Sultan*
8. Tomb of the Virgin* and Gardens of Gethsemane
9. House of Caiphas and Prison of Christ
10. Sanctuary of the Ascension* and Mount of Olives
11. Pool of Betheda
12. Ain Karim**
13. Basilica of the Nativity, Bethlehem* **
14. Milk Grotto, Bethlehem* **
15. Shepherds Field, Bethlehem* **

I to IX inclusive.
Stations of the Cross

MOSLEM

16. Tomb of Lazarus
17. El Burak esh-Sharif
18. Haram esh-Sharif (Mosque of Omar & Mosque of Aksa)
19. Mosque of the Ascension
20. Tomb of David (Nebi Daoud)

JEWISH

21. Tomb of Absalom
22. Ancient and Modern Synagogues
23. Bath of Rabbi Ishmael
24. Brook Siloam
25. Cemetery on Mount of Olives
26. Tomb of David
27. Tomb of Simon the Just
28. Tomb of Zachariah and other tombs in Kidron Valley
29. Wailing Wall*
30. Rachel's tomb* **

* Holy Place to which the Status Quo applies.
** Holy Places in international area of Jerusalem not shown on this map.

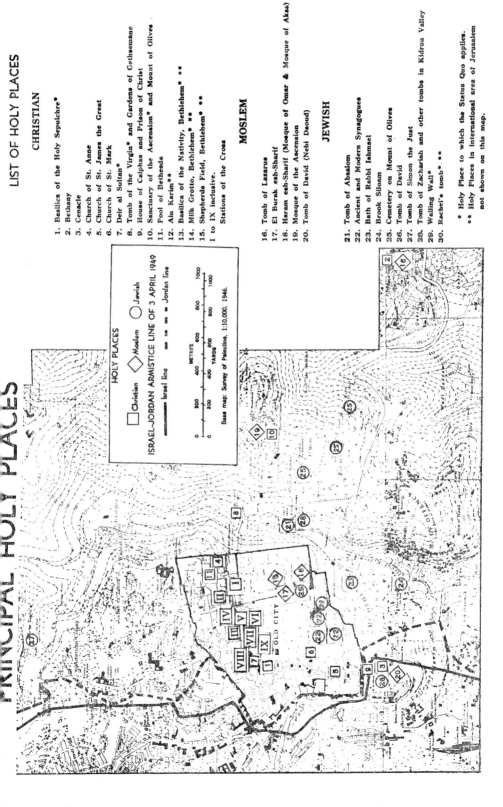

"The Jordanian attitude with regard to the preservation of the Arab character of Jerusalem has not changed."[5]

On the adoption of the partition resolution by the General Assembly, the Arabs in Palestine, actively abetted by the Governments of the Arab States, began disturbances to nullify it. Jerusalem was a principal target of the Arab attack. The city itself consists of the Old City within the walls, less than half a square mile in area, in which lie the Mosque of Omar (Dome of the Rock), the Church of the Holy Sepulchre and the Wailing Wall, sole remnant of the ancient Temple of Solomon, and, outside the walls, the New City, which has grown over the past hundred years, largely by Jewish construction and enterprise, to eleven square miles in area and with a population, in 1958, approaching 200,000, a thriving modern city like other large centers in Israel.

Of 30 principal Holy Places designated in the UN partition map (No. 229, November 1949), only two Christian sites and a Moslem dome are in the New City. All the others are in the Old City and its environs, and in nearby Bethlehem.

The Arab attacks first paralyzed and then split the municipal services. The Arabs sought to cut the only road by which food and fuel from the coastal plain could reach the New City. Convoys were ambushed; the pipe-line supplying Jerusalem with water was blown up; and the New City placed under siege. Arab artillery bombarded the New City for many weeks. Nearly 1,500 Jewish men, women and children were killed, and thousands more wounded. The health of many thousands of others was permanently affected by shortage of food and water, and disease.

The Jewish quarter in the Old City surrendered after a heroic defence. This hallowed precinct with its ancient synagogues and venerable academies and libraries was wholly demolished by the Arabs. The new Jewish city held out. A new track, "The Burma Road," was driven through the hills to by-pass Arab-held Latrun. Communications with Tel Aviv were restored and the siege was raised.

The New City had saved itself by its own exertions. No outside help had been vouchsafed, although the United Nations was in ineffectual session throughout that grim ordeal. The Security Council did not or could not act. The Trusteeship Council, charged to draft a statute for internationalized Jerusalem, referred the matter back to the General Assembly for fresh instructions, which were not forth-

[5] El Hayat, Beirut, January 22, 1957.

coming. Nothing was done to fulfil the resolution of November 29, 1947, which, among much else, enjoined on members of the United Nations "to ensure that order and peace reign in Jerusalem."

The Arab war and the siege of Jerusalem radically altered attitudes towards the future of the city. The Arabs were now divided. The Hashemite Kingdom of the Jordan had captured the Old City and was not prepared to yield it to any international regime or place its sacred sites under international supervision. Other Arab States, however, now pressed for internationalization, to a large degree as part of their maneuver to liquidate Jordan, which stood in the way of Egyp't expansionist ambitions. Bitter experience forced upon the Jews the conclusion that the security and very existence of the New City for which they had made so many sacrifices depended solely on its permanent inclusion within the State of Israel.

THE UNITED NATIONS AND JERUSALEM

At various times, the United Nations has considered the question of Jerusalem without taking action.

March, 1948:	Trusteeship Council completes Jerusalem statute. Because of Arab opposition its formal adoption is postponed.[6]
April 21, 1948:	Trusteeship Council asks General Assembly for further instructions, but receives none.[7]
July 29, 1948:	Trusteeship Council adjourns question indefinitely.[8]
September, 1949:	Palestine Conciliation Commission submits plan for division of Jerusalem into autonomous Israel and Arab zones, with a UN Commissioner responsible for protection of Holy Places.[9] Plan rejected by all Arab States and Israel.[10]
December 9, 1949:	General Assembly adopts resolution for territorial internationalization of Jerusalem,

[6] Report of the Trusteeship Council of the Third Session of the General Assembly, Doc. A/603.

[7] Ibid.

[8] Ibid.

[9] UN Doc. A/973. Item 18. Fourth Session, 12 September 1949. Communication from UN Palestine Conciliation Commission to Secretary-General Submitting Text of Draft Instrument.

[10] Official Records of the Fourth Session of the General Assembly, Plenary Meetings of the General Assembly, 20 September-10 December 1949.

supported by Soviets. Resolution opposed by U.S., Great Britain, Scandinavian countries, Jordan and Israel. U.S. representative warns Assembly that "resolution not only disregarded the interests of the inhabitants of Jerusalem, but also jeopardized the achievement of international rights to the area."[11]

December, 1950:	General Assembly considers Belgian and Swedish draft resolutions. Belgian resolution, following original partition plan, vigorously opposed by U.S. and Great Britain. Swedish resolution, providing for appointment of UN Commissioner to supervise Holy Places, accepted in principle by Israel and Jordan, after amendment by U.S. and Britain. Belgian resolution fails to get required majority. Swedish resolution not submitted to vote.[12]
December, 1952:	General Assembly rejects a Philippines amendment which sought to reinstate the principle of the internationalization of Jerusalem.

The majority support for internationalization, evident in 1949, was thus no longer in existence in 1952. The question of Jerusalem has not figured on the UN agenda since then.

ISRAEL AND JERUSALEM

For historic, economic, and political reasons, Israel claims the New City of Jerusalem as an integral part of her territory and as the capital of the State. Jerusalem has occupied a central position in the life of the Jewish people for over 3,000 years. It was the capital of David and Solomon, seat of the Holy Temple, and forum and academy for Jewry's prophets and sages. Jerusalem never capitulated to any conqueror. Its destruction by the Romans marked the end of Jewish statehood. The resurrection of the State of Israel made Jerusalem's restoration as its capital an inescapable event of history.

For countless generations of Jews, ascent to Jerusalem (aliyah), and residence within the city, were the holiest obligations. This attach-

11 Ibid., p. 579.
12 Official Records of the Fifth Session of the General Assembly, Plenary Meeting, UN Doc. A/2310. Report of the Ad Hoc Political Committee, Seventh Session, 15 December 1952.

ment is the central theme of Hebrew literature. For centuries it was the inspiration of Messianic movements among Jews in exile. Every proposal for Jewish national revival in their Homeland from Cyrus (6th century BCE to Napoleon 1800 CE) centered upon Jerusalem and its rebuilding.

There is strong evidence that an international regime for Jerusalem, of the kind transiently envisaged in the United Nations, would not be workable. Such regimes in other parts of the world (Danzig, Trieste, the Saar) have provoked harsh international conflict. The difficulties would be almost insurmountable in the case of Jerusalem, which is land-locked and wedged between two States which are not yet at peace. The proposed international city was not economically viable. The Old City was never self-supporting. The New City has become completely integrated into the fabric of Israel. It is supplied with water, food, and materials for its growing industry from other parts of the country. The Government has granted millions of dollars to foster its development. An index of its growing prosperity is given by statistics of population. The number, depleted by war, was just over 70,000 in the fall of 1948. It had risen to well beyond 150,000 by 1954 and is now approaching 200,000.

The revival has been brought about by new industrial development, housing schemes, extension of the agricultural hinterland, and the transfer to the city of Israel's State institutions. It is the seat of the President, Parliament (Knesset) Ministries, Supreme Court and Rabbinate.

The Government at its own expense has carried out costly repairs to Christian religious edifices damaged by enemy action.

The Government assumes full responsibility for the security of Holy Places in Israel territory and ensures free access and unhindered prayer. It affords opportunity for Christian pilgrims, whether local inhabitants or visitors, to cross into Jordan to worship at the Holy Places in the Old City and in Bethlehem.

In the course of the last eleven years, in fact immediately after the Israel-Jordan Armistice Agreement was signed, the Government made a number of conciliatory gestures with the hope that these would not be unilateral. Despite the provision of the Agreement that neither the Augusta Victoria Hospital in Jordan hands nor the Hadassah Hospital in Jewish hands should be re-activated on Mount Scopus, and that no military units should be stationed on either site, a few months after the Agreement Jordan military units were introduced and the Augusta Victoria Hospital was re-activated in the former site and all have been maintained despite protests by the Israel authorities. The Hadassah Hospital and Hebrew University have not only not been reactivated but supply convoys to maintain their caretaker staff and the few civilian police permitted under the Agree-have been continuously harried and have met with interference.

On the other hand, no Jews are allowed to visit the Wailing Wall, the Tomb of Rachel, the Cave of Machpelah, and the ancient Jewish cemetery on the Mount of Olives, which has been desecrated. These sites lie within the area of Jerusalem controlled by Jordan, which repudiates its undertaking in the Armistice Agreement with Israel to allow free access by Jews to their Holy Places in the Old City, to the ancient Jewish cemetery on the Mount of Olives, and to the Hebrew University and Hadassah Hospital on Mount Scopus.[13]

[13] Armistice Agreement, Article VIII (2).

CHAPTER XIV

Israel Looks to the Future

Israel's phenomenal development has been accomplished within the framework of the land area recognized by the parties to the Armistice Agreements of 1949 as constituting Israel's territory. At no time since those Armistice Agreements were signed has Israel sought any territorial expansion. Israel is content with its existing frontiers. Time and again Prime Minister David Ben Gurion has affirmed Israel's pacific intentions towards her neighbors. He told a press conference in Jerusalem on February 26, 1958: "We are willing to conclude not only a pact of non-aggression but even a pact of permanent peace on the basis of the territorial status quo." He had previously offered "to make peace with the Arab on the basis of existing borders for one hundred years."[1]

OF ITS TOTAL LAND AREA of slightly under 8,000 square miles, Israel, at the time writing, has but 1,500 under cultivation, of which almost one third is being irrigated. Some 2,500 square miles of the Negev and parts of the northern area of the country that have not yet been developed provide for a future increase of 147% in Israel's farmland. In other large sectors, at present considered unsuitable for agriculture, are an ever-expanding industrial and mining potential and the prerequisites for the continuous growth of urban population.

[1] Interviewed by United Press, May 13, 1953.

Israel, like other small countries, can provide economic opportunities and a rising standard of living for a relatively large population by applying modern scientific techniques to the utilization of its natural resources and the intensive development of local industry. This type of "development in depth" by the planned application of human resources, modern skills and technologies, and scientific knowledge is used by many other countries of relatively small area such as Britain, Switzerland, Belgium, the Netherlands and West Germany. With its present population numbering just over 2 million, and its past history of manufacturing absorptive capacity by transforming immigrants into productive citizens and a barren land into fertility. Israel in this light has ample room for millions of additional population.

All the countries mentioned above have population densities far higher than the approximately 240 persons per square mile in present-day Israel. The Netherlands, for example, has 850 persons per square mile; Belgium has 750; Britain has 550 and West Germany has 525. Some of these and many other countries of high density are not endowed with any over-abundance of raw mineral resources, but have yet managed to maintain a large and growing population at an increasing standard of living by applying modern methods to their agriculture, industry and commerce.

Within the Middle East itself, other countries have a higher population density than Israel. Lebanon, for example, with an unused agricultural potential of 63%, has a density of 355 per square mile. Egypt, with a present population of 24 millions, increasing by over half a million per year, has a total land area of 386,000 square miles but only 9,500 square miles under cultivation, with the possibility of adding not more than another 2,703 square miles of farm land (an increase of only 29%). The population density on the cultivable area of Egypt is already 1905 persons per square mile—the highest in the world—and this with an explosive birth rate which will double the population within the next two decades.

Countries with high educational and scientific standards can sustain large populations, the capacity to do so having little to do with physical space. Within the limits of its available water supplies, Israel has resources of soil and climate unequalled by any of the above mentioned countries of Europe, and is able to supply a larger proportion of its agricultural needs than any of them. Unlike other undeveloped countries, Israel has a large body of highly educated and skilled scientists, technicians and laborers. Its geographical position lends itself to the exploitation of international commerce. These technical advantages have already been recognized by other newly independent and under-developed countries of Asia and Africa, such as Burma, Ghana, etc., which are making use of Israel's technical and scientific skills and the experience gained as a pilot plant in desert reclamation to help stimulate their own development.

The history of Israel's first eleven years, and of the pioneer period of initial Jewish settlement which preceded it, has already demonstrated the country's capacity to expand its economy and provide livelihoods for its growing population. Since 1948 the population has more than doubled, by the immigration intake of 900,000 persons and the addition by natural increase of a further 300,000. Despite this great population growth in so short a time, the per capita income (not including aid received from abroad) is today higher than it was a decade ago. Between 1950 and 1956, while the population increased by nearly 50%, the Gross National Product, measured in constant prices, rose by 80%, while real Income Per Capita increased by 33%. During those years agricultural output rose by 118% while in the four years from 1952 to 1956 industrial output rose by 55%. The area under cultivation doubled in ten years, while land under irrigation nearly trebled, from 110,000 acres in 1949 to 308,000 acres today. Commodity exports rose nearly five fold between 1949 and 1956, while industrial output between 1948 and 1958 increased 800%. Israel's own production at present equals the total consumption requirements of its population, and its continued expansion will more than keep abreast of any foreseeable population growth by both natural increase and immigration. While it is true that a new immigrant, especially one without capital, represents a temporary burden on his host country, each newcomer is not only an additional mouth to feed and person to house. With the support of the entire population, by self-taxation and other efforts, and the good will and good citizenship shown by the country's newcomers, the immigrant speedily becomes a producer, himself helping to increase the agricultural, industrial or service production rate. In short, the immigrant in the course of months fast becomes an absorber of further immigrants.

With space for internal expansion and a rise in productivity rate faster than consumption, by a growing population, Israel faces the choice not of higher living standards or further immigration absorption but of both. The ratio between them is determined by many factors, not the least of which is the volume of pressure by Jews throughout the world for immediate immigration. Whilst the doors of Israel, according to its Law of the Return, are perpetually and unrestrictedly open to such immigration, this pressure varies according to time and circumstance.

The Law of Return,[2] 5710-1950, states that "every Jew has the right to come to this country as an immigrant." It is one of, if not actually *the,* most fundamental law of the State of Israel reflecting the very raison d'etre of the Jewish State. For it was for this purpose, the ingathering of the Jewish people from exile, the solution of the Jewish problem of homelessness, that Israel was established by its pioneers.

The Law of Return is complemented by a second law, the Nationality Law[3], 5712-1952, which states that "every 'oleh' (Jewish immigrant) under the Law of Return, 5710-1950, shall become an Israeli national."

The most optimistic view of Israel's leaders is that by immigration intake and natural increase the population of the country will in the next ten years not exceed much more than three million. Such an increase of population would remain well below the average increase in Israel's output, thus insuring work opportunities and income for the anticipated population increment, as well as insuring progress towards self-sufficiency within its existing borders. Small as its land area may be, Israel is content to abide within it, seeking to revive the Negev desert and other waste areas, returning them to their ancient fruitfulness. Coupled with intensive developments of agriculture, industry and services, a steadily rising standard of living on the basis of an expanding population is thus entirely feasible. No internal pressures exist, in terms of land shortage, restrictions on productive capacity, or explosive population density to cause her to deviate from its consistent policy of peace towards its neighbors on the basis of existing frontiers.

Indeed, Israel's vested interest in peace has been reflected by a succession of offers to its Arab neighbors all of a unilateral nature, during the first eleven years of its sovereign existence. Despite the fact that none of them has met with any pacific response, but in fact all have either been studiously ignored or been received with renewed invective and aggression, Israel persistently continues with its efforts at reducing tension in the area and creating the conditions

[2] Reshumot, *Sefer Ha Hukkim,* No. 51 of 6 July 1950, p. 159.

[3] Passed by the Knesset on the 6th Nissan, 5712 (1 April 1952): the Bill was published in *Hatza'ot Chok,* No. 93 of 22 Heshvan, 5712 (21 November 1951), p. 22.

for a stable and permanent peace. But a few of these many peace overtures and offers to her Arab neighbors are quoted hereunder:

> "We extend the hand of peace and good-neighborliness to all the States around us and to their peoples, and we call upon them to cooperate in mutual helpfulness with the independent Jewish nation in its land. The State of Israel is prepared to make its contribution in a concerted effort for the advancement of the entire Middle East."[4]

> "The Government of Israel has consistently declared its readiness to enter into direct negotiations with its neighbors for the peaceful settlement of all outstanding questions. It is the firm conviction of my Government that peace can be obtained only by direct negotiations, with or without international assistance."[5]

> "We are prepared, and indeed, willing, at any time to negotiate peace with the countries bound to us by an Armistice Agreement in order to develop these Agreements either into final peace settlements or into any progressive development of more peaceful relations."[6]

> "If there is any Egyptian statesman who is ready to meet me to consider ways and means for the improvement of relations between Israel and the Arab States, I am ready at any time or place."[7]

> "The Government will work untiringly for the achievement of peaceful relations and cooperation between Israel and the Arab States."[8]

> "The obvious and essential need for our area is the conclusion of peace treaties placing the relationship between neighboring States on a permanently normal footing."[9]

> "We fervently hope that our neighbors will come to realize the futility of their efforts to destroy Israel and that they will at last grasp the hand of peace that it stretches out to them."[10]

Besides these reiterated offers to negotiate a peaceful settlement of differences, Israel has held out specific advantages to the Arabs. These include the use by Jordan of the port of Haifa; compensation

[4] Declaration of Independence, May 14, 1948.

[5] Moshe Sharett, Israel Minister for Foreign Affairs, in the General Assembly, December 14, 1950.

[6] Ambassador Abba Eban, in the Security Council, November 3, 1954.

[7] Prime Minister David Ben Gurion (then Minister of Defense) interviewed by United Press, July 24, 1955.

[8] Prime Minister David Ben Gurion, addressing the Knesset, Jerusalem, November 2, 1955.

[9] Foreign Minister Golda Meir, in the General Assembly, October 7, 1957.

[10] Prime Minister David Ben Gurion, *New York Herald Tribune,* March 12, 1958.

to refugees for abandoned lands; release of blocked refugee accounts (actually effected on April 10, 1952); overland communication facilities between Egypt and Jordan.

Step-by-step stages for the evolution of Arab-Israel peace within the framework of the Armistice Agreements were outlined to the General Assembly in 1954 by Ambassador Abba Eban.

Invariably, the Arab response to these offers has been renewed threats of belligerency:

Gamal Abdel Nasser, President of the United Arab Republic:

"Israel is an artificial State which must disappear." (In an interview with the Greek newspaper, "Kathimeriri," May 8, 1954.)

Nasser again:

"The war between us and Zionism has not yet ended, and perhaps has not yet even begun. For us, this war of tomorrow or of the near future means the ending of a disgrace, the realization of a hope and the regaining of rights." (From Nasser's introduction to the book "This is Zionism," Cairo, 1955.)

Anwar Al-Sadat, Egyptian Minister of State:

"Wait and see, Ben Gurion! Soon the strength and willpower of the Arabs will be proven to you. Egypt and the Arab nations will teach you a lesson and quiet you forever. Egypt will grind you to the dust." (Reported in "Al Goumhouriya," official Government newspaper, Cairo, April 8, 1956.)

Continuous incitement against Israel at home, threats and promises to destroy Israel, an arms buildup justified by the openly proclaimed aim to expel Israel's population from the area and "liberate" this "part of the Arab homeland," are not conducive to a pacific reaction by the Arab leaders to Israel's successive peace overtures.

CHAPTER XV

Conclusion

THE preceding pages have drawn attention to recurring points of issue between the Arab States and Israel. No issue is insoluble if both sides tackle it in a spirit of good will. Israel's position is plain. She has repeatedly expressed a readiness to meet the Arab States, jointly or singly, to discuss ways and means of settling matters in dispute. No progress can be made if only one side is prepared to negotiate, and so far the Arab States have uncompromisingly declined to recognize Israel's standing as a permanent factor in the Middle East. For the time being, then, Israel must pursue alone those plans for development which, if extended to the whole region, would be of inestimable benefit to all its inhabitants.

Arab-Israel relations constitute but one of the issues, by no means the most serious or the most difficult to solve, confronting the Middle East scene. It is often overlooked that the region is peopled only in part by the Arab States, and that the majority of its inhabitants consist of other nationalities. The Middle East, as defined in the general practice of the United Nations, is inhabited by some 60,000,000 Arabs, taking language as the broadest criterion, and 75,000,000 non-Arabs. There is a non-Arab Middle East extending from Turkey and Iran through Israel to Ethiopia; and if the area is enlarged to include Afganistan and Pakistan, then the predominantly non-Arab character of the region is even more manifest. Within this context, official declarations, particularly by the U.A.R., about a continuous area stretching between the Atlantic Ocean and the Persian Gulf as the inheritance of any one nation must be regarded as an offense against international peace as well as a distortion of history, geography and law. But even within the narrower context of those Middle Eastern countries which speak the same Arabic language, attempts of Nasser's Egypt to dominate the whole region and bring it under his sway are no more justified historically than, for example, an attempt by a South American State to assert its hegemony over the other Spanish-speaking republics of that continent. The resistances of Jordan, Lebanon, Iraq, Sudan and Tunisia to such attempts at subjection, in their struggle to preserve their own identity and independence have not only preoccupied the region and the world community of nations in latter years, but have also, at the same time, placed the area of conflict between Israel and the Arab States in its proper modest dimensions.

Enmeshed in this inter-Arab conflict is the historic rivalry between Egypt and Iraq for leadership, the clash of interests between the haves (oil producing countries) and the have-nots, aggravated by a prevalence of poverty, disease and ignorance in all of them, that generates inflammable resentment and extremism. There is another tug of war, again historic in certain of its aspects at least, between East and West, which involves the Middle East in the global tensions between these two blocs.

All these problems and many others have for long, and independently of the Arab-Israel dispute, upset regional tranquility. Though their peaceful solution would undoubtedly enhance the prospects of an Arab-Israel settlement, such a settlement, only given Arab willingness to negotiate one, is not necessarily dependent on their being solved.

There is, in fact, no inherent contradiction between the legitimate interests of Israel and her Arab neighbors. Israel has no quarrel with the legitimate aspirations of the Arab peoples to attain national independence and to become masters of their own economic and political destinies. Israel welcomes every forward step those peoples take along the road of social advancement, believing that any improvement in their conditions of life will tend to slacken tensions that are often artificially prolonged in the interests of domestic politics.

Legitimate aspirations, however, in accordance with the United Nations Charter, must mean for all nationalisms and States in the Middle East recognition and respect for the sacred principle of sovereignty. Federations of any kind must be based upon the voluntary decision of States concerned and must inherently imply the right of all States in the region to join or refrain from joining them, or enter into any free association based on cooperation.

Recognition of this fundamental principle of sovereignty is the essential difference between legitimate and illegitimate nationalism in the Middle East or elsewhere. Within its context all problems of the region, including those outstanding between Israel and the Arab States, can be solved. None of the problems discussed in this volume are outside the compass of such a solution. In fact, the inherent interest of the peoples of the Arab States in social progress, national self-determination and political democracy are totally harmonious with the similarly inherent interests of the Jewish people in its ancestral Homeland. For both peoples, as all others, is the stark choice of peaceful cooperation or destructive strife. Israel's choice of cooperation must surely and inevitably be matched, if not at first out of altruism, at least ultimately in self-interest, by a similar choice by the Arab States.

Appendix 1

ENDORSEMENT AND ADOPTION OF THE BALFOUR DECLARATION BY THE ALLIED AND ASSOCIATED POWERS OF THE FIRST WORLD WAR

The Palestine Royal Commission of 1937 found and stated as a fact that

"The text of the Declaration had been submitted to President Wilson (of the United States of America) and had been approved by him before its publication. On the 14th February and the 9th May, 1918, the French and Italian Governments publicly endorsed it." (Report, Royal Commission, 1937 (Comd.5479) p. 22)

The other Allies of the First World War likewise endorsed the Declaration shortly thereafter (Hanna, "British Policy in Palestine", p. 36).

Appendix 2

TO WHOM WAS THE PLEDGE OF THE BALFOUR DECLARATION MADE?*

Prime Minister MacDonald, in his official letter on behalf of the British Government to Dr. Weizmann, of 13th February, 1931, stated that:

"His Majesty's Government . . . recognizes that the undertaking of the Mandate (embodying the pledge of the Balfour Declaration) is an undertaking to the Jewish people and not only to the Jewish population of Palestine."

Mr. Winston Churchill, who was an important member of the Government which issued the Balfour Declaration, used the following language upon this subject in his address in the House of Commons on May 23, 1939 (Parliamentary Debates, Vol. 347, No. 108, Columns 2181-2182):

"To whom was the pledge of the Balfour Declaration made? It was not made to the Jews of Palestine, it was not made to those who were actually living in Palestine. It was made to world Jewry and in particular to the Zionist associations. It was in consequence of and on the basis of this pledge that we received important help in the War, and that after the War we received from the Allied and Associated Powers the Mandate for Palestine. The pledge of a home of refuge, of an asylum, was not made to the Jews in Palestine but to the Jews outside Palestine, to that vast, unhappy mass of scattered, persecuted, wandering Jews whose intense, unchanging, unconquerable desire has been for a National Home—to quote the words to which my right hon. Friend the Prime Minister subscribed in the Memorial which he and others sent to us:

> 'the Jewish people who have through centuries of dispersion and persecution patiently awaited the hour of its restoration to its ancestral home.'

* Book of Documents submitted to the General Assembly of the United Nations (The Jewish Agency for Palestine, New York, May 1947), pp. 1-11.

Those are the words. They were the people outside, not the people in. It is not with the Jews in Palestine that we have now or at any future time to deal, but with world Jewry, with Jews all over the world. That is the pledge which was given, and that is the pledge which we are asked to break, for how can this pledge be kept, I want to know, if in five years' time the National Home is to be barred and no more Jews are to be allowed in without the permission of the Arabs?"

Field-Marshal Smuts, who as a member of the War Cabinet which issued the Balfour Declaration was one of its chief architects and authors, said as follows in a broadcast speech on November 1, 1941:

"The Allies promised to the Jewish people, after an exile of almost two thousand years, that a National Home would be founded for them in their ancient Homeland.

"Was it a vow made in an hour of sore trial? Was it a vision of a future such as sometimes appears at the darkest hour? Was it an act of faith such as made Abraham willing to sacrifice his only son in his extreme old age?

"Whatever it was, the step was taken. The document was signed with the approval of the British, the French, and the American Governments. It was at least a great gesture before history. And finally, it was embodied in the Peace Treaty, and the promise to Abraham had at last become a part of the international law of the world. The Balfour Declaration was not a mere accident, a mere eccentricity of the Great War, but in its large historic setting and in its solemn legal form is one of the greatest acts of history. To the oppressed Jews it opened up the fulfilment of the visions which their poets had embodied in immortal language. Think of that poignant Psalm of exile: 'If I forget theee, O Jerusalem, may my right hand forget her cunning.' Think of that still more moving Psalm of return: 'When the Lord turned again to the captivity of Zion, we were like them that dream.'

"The promise of a National Home—the Palestine Mandate—seemed to be the answer to the prayers and the tears of a people who had suffered as no other, who for long ages had become the scapegoat of history . . .

"Since these promising beginnings there have been setbacks. Doubt and contention once more have arisen in high places in Palestine, though the hard and good work has gone on without pause. Over Europe a new eclipse has overtaken the Jewish race. Beginning in Nazi Germany, a new horror of persecution started which in one degree and another has spread to many other countries. The lassitude and frustration which have overtaken post-war Europe seem to have found a scapegoat once more in the Jews. Uprooted with unprecedented suffering from their old homes, they found immigration laws everywhere barring their escape to other countries. New ghettos are arising which in their misery and despair outrival the record of the Middle Ages. Humanity is ashamed and disgraced as perhaps never before in the records of civilisation. The new hope is perishing in a despair darker than death. Such is the change which has come over the Jewish cause in the last two decades. The calamities which have overtaken the post-war world generally have reached a climax in the anti-Semitic movement, surpassing in dimensions and intensity anything known in history.

"The case of the Balfour Declaration thus has become overwhelmingly stronger. Instead of the horror of new ghettos in the twentieth century, let us carry out our promise and open up the National Home. The case has become one not merely of promises and international law but for the conscience of mankind. We dare not fold our hands without insulting the human spirit itself."

Area of Jewish National Home

The field in which the Jewish National Home was to be established under the Balfour Declaration, as stated and understood at the time the Declaration was issued, was the whole of historic Palestine on both sides of the Jordan. This was specifically found to be the fact by the Palestine Royal Commission, in these words (Palestine Royal Commission Report, July, 1937, Cmd. 5479, p. 38):

"The field in which the Jewish National Home was to be established was understood, at the time of the Balfour Declaration, to be the whole of historic Palestine, and the Zionists were seriously disappointed when Trans-Jordan was cut away from that field under Article 25" (of the later Mandate).

Mr. Leopold S. Amery, one of the Secretaries to the British War Cabinet in 1917 and 1918, and thereafter Under Secretary and Secretary of State for the Colonies, gave the following testimony upon this subject to the Anglo-American Committee of Inquiry in January, 1946 (Transcript of Wednesday, January 30, 1946, p. 112):

"Q. (by Mr. Buxton) The Trans-Jordan was definitely in the minds of the framers of the Balfour Declaration when the Declaration was issued? There is no question of that. Palestine embraced Trans-Jordan in the concept of the persons who framed the Balfour Declaration?

"A. Yes. To the best of my recollection, certainly at the time the Cabinet decided on the Balfour Declaration they regarded Trans-Jordan as being within Palestine. They also, I think, regarded it, as probably the whole thing was experimental, that there would be eventually a Jewish majority over the whole of Palestine.

"I always assumed that the particular references to not infringing the civil or religious liberties of the Arab population were not so much a safeguard against the British Government infringing those liberties against the possibility of a Jewish majority, but a Jewish state infringing those liberties. Therefore, at the time that possibility of a Jewish majority over the whole of the Larger Palestine was, I think, envisaged. Lloyd George has, I believe, in evidence definitely stated that some time ago."

National Home Meant Jewish State

The phrase "the establishment in Palestine of a national home for the Jewish people" was intended and understood by all concerned to mean at the time of the Balfour Declaration that Palestine would ultimately become a "Jewish Commonwealth" or a "Jewish State", if only Jews came and settled there in sufficient numbers. Thus, President Wilson stated on March 3, 1919:

> "I am persuaded that the Allied Nations, with the fullest concurrence of our own Government and people, are agreed that in Palestine shall be laid the foundations of a Jewish Commonwealth."

Mr. David Lloyd George, who was Prime Minister of the Government which issued the Balfour Declaration, quoted with complete approval, in his testimony before the Palestine Royal Commission of 1937, the following explanation by Mr. Balfour himself when proposing the Declaration to the Cabinet for adoption:

"As to the meaning of the words 'National Home', to which the Zionists attach so much importance, he understood it to mean some form of British, American or other protectorate, under which full facilities would be given to the Jews to work out their own salvation and to build up, by means of education, agriculture, and industry, a real centre of national culture and focus of national life. It did not necessarily involve the early establishment of an independent Jewish State, which was a matter of gradual development in accordance with the ordinary laws of political evolution."

Mr. Lloyd George then proceeded to give the following testimony upon this subject before the Royal Commission on his own account (cf. Report, Royal Commission, p. 24):

". . . there could be no doubt as to what the Cabinet then had in their minds. It was not their idea that a Jewish State should be set up immediately by the Peace Treaty . . . On the other hand, it was contemplated that when the time arrived for according representative institutions to Palestine, if the Jews had meanwhile responded to the opportunity afforded them . . . and had become a definitive majority of the inhabitants, then Palestine would thus become a Jewish Commonwealth. The notion that Jewish immigration would have to be artificially restricted in order to ensure that the Jews should be a permanent minority never entered into the heads of anyone engaged in framing the policy. That would have been regarded as unjust and as a fraud on the people to whom we were appealing."

Mr. Winston Churchill used these words upon this subject in 1920 ("Illustrated Sunday Herald" of London of February 8, 1920):

"If, as may well happen, there should be created in our own lifetime by the banks of the Jordan a Jewish State under the protection of the British Crown which might comprise three or four millions of Jews, an event will have occurred in the history of the world which would from every point of view be beneficial, and would be especially in harmony with the truest interests of the British Empire."

The Palestine Royal Commission of 1937 summarized the following additional evidence upon this subject in its Report (pp. 24-25):

"General Smuts, who had been a member of the Imperial War Cabinet when the Declaration was published, speaking at Johannesburg on the 3rd November, 1919, foretold an increasing stream of Jewish immigration into Palestine and 'in generations to come a great Jewish State rising there once more'. Lord Robert Cecil in 1917, Sir Herbert Samuel in 1919, and Mr. Winston Churchill in 1920 spoke or wrote in terms that could only mean that they contemplated the eventual establishment of a Jewish State. Leading British newspapers were equally explicit in their comments on the Declaration."

American Understanding of Balfour Declaration

The American understanding of the intent and purpose of the Balfour Declaration is clearly deducible from the following Outline of Tentative Report and Recommendations of the Intelligence Section of the American Delegation to the Peace Conference, in accordance with instructions, for the President and the Plenipotentiaries, January 21, 1919 (David Hunte Miller, "My Diary at the Conference of Paris", Vol. IV, pp. 263-264):

"26. PALESTINE.

It is recommended:

1) *That there be established a separate state of Palestine.*

2) *That this state be placed under Great Britain as a mandatory of the League of Nations.*

3) *That the Jews be invited to return to Palestine and settle there, being assured by the Conference of all proper assistance in so doing that may be consistent with the protection of the personal (especially the religious) and the property rights of the non-Jewish population, and being further assured that it will be the policy of the League of Nations to recognize Palestine as a Jewish state as soon as it is a Jewish state in fact.*

4) *That the holy places and religious rights of all creeds in Palestine be placed under the protection of the League of Nations and its mandatory.*

DISCUSSION

1) It is recommended that there be established a separate state of Palestine.

The separation of the Palestinian area from Syria finds justification in the religious experience of mankind. The Jewish and Christian churches were born in Palestine, and Jerusalem was for long years, at different periods, the capital of each. And while the relation of the Mohammedans to Palestine is not so intimate, from the beginning they have regarded Jerusalem as a holy place. Only by establishing Palestine as a separate state can justice be done to these great facts.

As drawn upon the map, the new state would control its own source of water power and irrigation, on Mount Hermon in the east to the Jordan; a feature of great importance since the success of the new state would depend upon the possibilities of agricultural development.

2) It is recommended that this state be placed under Great Britain as a mandatory of the League of Nations.

Palestine would obviously need wise and firm guidance. Its population is without political experience, is racially composite, and could easily become distracted by fanaticism and bitter religous dfferences.

The success of Great Britain in dealing with similar situations, her relation to Egypt, and her administrative achievements since General Allenby freed Palestine from the Turk, all indicate her as the logical mandatory.

3) It is recommended that the Jews be invited to return to Palestine and settle there, being assured by the Conference of all proper assistance in so doing that may be consistent with the protection of the personal (especially the religious) and the property rights of the non-Jewish population, and being further assured that it will be the policy of the League of Nations to recognize Palestine as a Jewish state as soon as it is a Jewish state in fact.

It is right that Palestine should become a Jewish state if the Jews, being given the full opportunity, make it such. It was the cradle and home of their vital race, which has made large spiritual contributions to mankind, and is the only land in which they can hope to find a home of their own; they being in this last respect unique among significant peoples.

At present, however, the Jews form barely a sixth of the total population of 700,000 in Palestine, and whether they are to form a majority, or even a plurality, of the population in the future state remains uncertain. Palestine, in short, is far from being a Jewish country now. England, as mandatory, can be relied on to give the Jews the privileged position they should have without sacrificing the rights of non-Jews.

4) It is recommended that the holy places and religious rights of all creeds in Palestine be placed under the protection of the League of Nations and its mandatory.

The basis for this recommendation is self evident."

Appendix 3

TREATY OF PEACE BETWEEN THE PRINCIPAL ALLIED POWERS AND TURKEY

Sèvres, August 10, 1920

Article 95

"The High Contracting Parties agree to entrust, by application of the provisions of Article 22, the administration of Palestine, within such boundaries as may be determined by the Principal Allied Powers, to a Mandatory to be selected by the said Powers. The Mandatory will be responsible for putting into effect the declaration originally made on November 2, 1917, by the British Government, and adopted by the other Allied Powers, in favour of the establishment in Palestine of a national home for the Jewish people, it being clearly understood that nothing shall be done which may prejudice the civil and religious rights of existing non-Jewish communities in Palestine or the rights and political status enjoyed by Jews in any other country."

Appendix 4

ACCORD AND DECISION OF THE CONFERENCE OF THE PRINCIPAL ALLIED POWERS AT SAN REMO, 1920

At the San Remo Conference held in April 1920, the Principal Allied Powers decided that the Mandate for the government of Palestine should be entrusted to Great Britain and that

"The Mandatory Power will be responsible for putting into effect the Declaration originally made on November 2nd, 1917, by the British Government in favour of the establishment of a National Home for the Jewish people, subject to the conditions included in the Declaration itself" (Duke of Devonshire, House of Lords, 27th June, 1923).

Appendix 5

AGREEMENT BETWEEN EMIR FEISAL AND DR. WEIZMANN, JANUARY 3, 1919*

His Royal Highness the Emir Feisal, representing and acting on behalf of the Arab Kingdom of Hedjaz, and Dr. Chaim Weizmann, representing and acting on behalf of the Zionist Organisation, mindful of the racial kinship and ancient bonds existing between the Arabs and the Jewish people, and realising that the surest means of working out the consummation of their national aspirations is through the closest possible collaboration in the development of the Arab State and Palestine, and being desirous further of confirming the good understanding which exists between them, have agreed upon the following Articles:

Article I

The Arab State and Palestitne in all their relations and undertakings shall be controlled by the most cordial goodwill and understanding, and to this end Arab and Jewish duly accredited agents shall be established and maintained in the respective territories.

Article II

Immediately following the completion of the deliberations of the Peace Conference, the definite boundaries between the Arab State and Palestine shall be determined by a Commission to be agreed upon by the parties hereto.

Article III

In the establishment of the Constitution and Administration of Palestine all such measures shall be adopted as will afford the fullest

* Book of Documents submitted to the General Assembly of the United Nations (Jewish Agency for Palestine, New York, May 1947).

guarantees for carrying into effect the British Government's Declaration of the 2nd of November, 1917.

Article IV

All necessary measures shall be taken to encourage and stimulate immigration of Jews into Palestine on a large scale, and as quickly as possible to settle Jewish immigrants upon the land through closer settlement and intensive cultivation of the soil. In taking such measures the Arab peasant and tenant farmers shall be protected in their rights, and shall be assisted in forwarding their economic development.

Article V

No regulation nor law shall be made prohibiting or interfering in any way with the free exercise of religion; and further the free exercise and enjoyment of religious profession and worship without discrimination or preference shall forever be allowed. No religious test shall ever be required for the exercise of civil or political rights.

Article VI

The Mohammedan Holy Places shall be under Mohammedan control.

Article VII

The Zionist Organisation proposes to send to Palestine a Commission of experts to make a survey of the economic possibilities of the country, and to report upon the best means for its development. The Zionist Organisation will place the aforementioned Commission at the disposal of the Arab State for the purpose of a survey of the economic possibilities of the Arab State and to report upon the best means for its development. The Zionist Organisation will use its best efforts to assist the Arab State in providing the means for developing the natural resources and economic possibilities thereof.

Article VIII

The parties hereto agree to act in complete accord and harmony on all matters embraced herein before the Peace Conference.

Article IX

Any matters of dispute which may arise between the contracting parties shall be referred to the British Government for arbitration.

Given under our hand at London, England, the third day of January, one thousand nine hundred and nineteen.

CHAIM WEIZMANN
FEISAL IBN-HUSSEIN

Reservation by the Emir Feisal

If the Arabs are established as I have asked in my manifesto of January 4th addressed to the British Secretary of State for Foreign Affairs, I will carry out what is written in this agreement. If changes are made, I cannot be answerable for failing to carry out this agreement.

FEISAL IBN-HUSSEIN

Appendix 6

FEISAL-FRANKFURTER CORRESPONDENCE

Delegation Hedjazienne, Paris, March 3, 1919

Dear Mr. Frankfurter:

I want to take this opportunity of my first contact with American Zionists to tell you what I have often been able to say to Dr. Weizmann in Arabia and Europe.

We feel that the Arabs and Jews are cousins in race, having suffered similar oppressions at the hands of powers stronger than themselves, and by a happy coincidence have been able to take the first steps towards the attainment of their national ideals together.

We Arabs, especially the educated among us, look with the deepest sympathy on the Zionist movement. Our deputation here in Paris is fully acquainted with the proposals submitted yesterday by the Zionist Organisation to the Peace Conference, and we regard them as moderate and proper. We will do our best, in so far as we are concerned, to help them through: we will wish the Jews a most hearty welcome home.

With the chiefs of your movement, especially with Dr. Weizmann, we have had and continue to have the closest relations. He has been a great helper of our cause, and I hope the Arabs may soon be in a position to make the Jews some return for their kindness. We are working together for a reformed and revived Near East, and our two movements complete one another. The Jewish movement is national and not imperialistic. Our movement is national and not imperialistic, and there is room in Syria for us both. Indeed I think that neither can be a real success without the other.

People less informed and less responsible than our leaders and yours, ignoring the need for cooperation of the Arabs and Zionists, have been trying to exploit the local difficulties that must necessarily arise in Palestine in the early stages of our movements. Some of them have, I am afraid, misrepresented your aims to the Arab peasantry, and our aims to the Jewish peasantry, with the result that interested parties have been able to make capital out of what they call our differences.

I wish to give you my firm conviction that these differences are not on questions of principle, but on matters of detail such as must inevitably occur in every contact of neighboring peoples, and as are easily adjusted by mutual goodwill. Indeed nearly all of them will disappear with fuller knowledge.

I look forward, and my people with me look forward, to a future in which we will help you and you will help us, so that the countries in which we are mutually interested may once again take their places in the community of civilised peoples of the world.

Believe me,

Yours sincerely,

(sgd) FEISAL

5th March, 1919

Appendix 7

JOINT RESOLUTION OF THE CONGRESS OF THE UNITED STATES ADOPTED JUNE 30, 1922, AND SIGNED BY PRESIDENT HARDING ON SEPTEMBER 20, 1922*

"Whereas the Jewish people have for many centuries believed in and yearned for the rebuilding of their ancient homeland; and

"Whereas owing to the outcome of the World War and their part therein, the Jewish people are to be enabled to recreate and reorganize a national home in the land of their fathers, which will give to the House of Israel its long-denied opportunity to re-establish a fruitful Jewish life and culture in the ancient Jewish land: therefore be it

"Resolved by the Senate and House of Representatives of the United States of America in Congress assembled, that the United States of America favors the establishment in Palestine of a national home for the Jewish people, it being clearly understood that nothing shall be done which may prejudice the civil and religious rights of Christian and all other non-Jewish communities in Palestine, and that the holy places and religious buildings and sites in Palestine shall be adequately protected." (Congressional Record, June 30th, 1922)

* U.S. Congressional Record, 67th Cong., 2nd Session (June 30, 1922), p. 9800.

APPENDIX 8

LEAGUE OF NATIONS MANDATE FOR PALESTINE*

[The following preamble and articles of the League of Nations Mandate for Palestine are its fundamental clauses.]

The Council of the League of Nations:

Whereas the Principal Allied Powers have agreed, for the purpose of giving effect to the provisions of Article 22 of the Covenant of the League of Nations, to entrust to a mandatory selected by the said Powers the administration of the territory of Palestine, which formerly belonged to the Turkish Empire, within such boundaries as may be fixed by them; and

Whereas the Principal Allied Powers have also agreed that the Mandatory should be responsible for putting into effect the declaration originally made on November 2nd, 1917, by the Government of His Britannic Majesty, and adopted by the said Powers, in favour of the establishment in Palestine of a national home for the Jewish people, it being clearly understood that nothing should be done which might prejudice the civil and religious rights of existing non-Jewish communities in Palestine, or the rights and political status enjoyed by Jews in any other country; and

Whereas recognition has thereby been given to the historical connection of the Jewish people with Palestine and to the grounds for reconstituting their national home in that country; and

Whereas the Principal Allied Powers have selected His Britannic Majesty as the Mandatory for Palestine; and

Whereas the mandate in respect of Palestine has been formulated in the following terms and submitted to the Council of the League for approval; and

* Approved by the Council of the League of Nations on July 24, 1922. Went into effect on September 29, 1923. See Great Britain, Parliamentary Papers 1922, Cmd. 1785, pp. 1-11.

Whereas His Britannic Majesty has accepted the mandate in respect of Palestine and undertaken to exercise it on behalf of the League of Nations in conformity with the following provisions; and

Whereas by the afore-mentioned Article 22 (paragraph 8), it is provided that the degree of authority, control or administration to be exercised by the Mandatory, not having been previously agreed upon by the Members of the League, shall be explicitly defined by the Council of the League of Nations;

Confirming the said mandate defines its terms as follows:

Article 1

The Mandatory shall have full powers of legislation and of administration, save as they may be limited by the terms of this mandate.

Article 2

The Mandatory shall be responsible for placing the country under such political, administrative and economic conditions as will secure the establishment of the Jewish national home, as laid down in the preamble, and the development of self-governing institutions, and also for safeguarding the civil and religious rights of all the inhabitants of Palestine, irrespective of race and religion.

Article 3

The Mandatory shall, so far as circumstances permit, encourage local autonomy.

Article 4

An appropriate Jewish agency shall be recognized as a public body for the purpose of advising and co-operating with the Administration of Palestine in such economic, social and other matters as may affect the establishment of the Jewish national home and the interests of the Jewish population in Palestine, and, subject always to the control of the Administration, to assist and take part in the development of the country.

The Zionist Organisation, so long as its organisation and constitution are in the opinion of the Mandatory appropriate, shall be recognised as such agency. It shall take steps in consultation with His Britannic Majesty's Government to secure the cooperation of all Jews who are willing to assist in the establishment of the Jewish national home.

Article 5

The Mandatory shall be responsible for seeing that no Palestine territory shall be ceded or leased to, or in any way placed under the control of, the Government of any foreign Power.

Article 6

The Administration of Palestine, while ensuring that the rights and position of other sections of the population are not prejudiced, shall facilitate Jewish immigration under suitable conditions and shall encourage, in cooperation with the Jewish agency referred to in Article 4, close settlement by Jews on the land, including State lands and waste lands not required for public purposes.

Article 27

The consent of the Council of the League of Nations is required for any modification of the terms of this mandate.

From the

Certified true copy:

For the Secretary-General
RAPPARD
Director of the Mandates Section

Appendix 9

VIEWS OF U. S. CONGRESS ON ESTABLISHMENT OF JEWISH COMMONWEALTH

Mr. Wagner, from the Committee on Foreign Relations, submitted the following report (to accompany S.Con.Res.44)

The Committee on Foreign Relations which has had under consideration several resolutions relating to the restoration of Palestine as a homeland for the Jewish people reports favorably a concurrent resolution (S. Con. Res. 44) expressing the policy of the Congress with respect to the restoration of Palestine as a homeland for the Jewish people, and recommend that the concurrent resolution do pass.

The plight of the Jews in Europe and the indefinite status of Palestine formed the subject of a number of resolutions introduced in recent years and referred to the Foreign Relations Committee. Most recently, three proposals were submitted. The first was Senate Concurrent Resolution No. 37 introduced by Mr. Myers and Mr. Tobey on October 2, 1945. The second was Senate Joint Resolution No. 112 introduced by Mr. Wagner, for himself, Mr. Taft, and Mr. Walsh, on October 26. The third was a proposal in the form of an amendment to Senate Joint Resolution No. 112 offered in the Senate Foreign Relations Committee by Mr. Guffey on November 19, 1945. A subcommittee consisting of Mr. Green, chairman; Mr. Tunnell; Mr. Hatch; Mr. Austin; and Mr. Wiley was appointed to consider these proposals. The subcommittee had a number of meetings, at two of which the Secretary of State was present. The matter was also considered by the full committee at several meetings, at one of which the Secretary of State was present.

Your committee, while cognizant of the appointment of a joint Anglo-American committee of inquiry into the subject and while it commends the President for his interest in the matter, feels at the same time that it is appropriate and timely for the Congress to give expression to its views on the need for the restoration of Palestine as the Jewish national homeland.

Accordingly, the Foreign Relations Committee, by an almost unanimous vote, has decided to report favorably an original concurrent resolution.

In the opinion of your committee the language of this resolution reflects a long series of authoritative expressions of American policy and the views of the American people on the subject of Palestine.

This policy and these views go back to January 21, 1919, when the following recommendation was made by the intelligence section of the United States delegation to the Paris Peace Conference:

That the Jews be invited to return to Palestine and settle there, being assured by the Peace Conference of all proper assistance in so doing that may be consistent with the protection of the personal (especially the religious) and property rights of the non-Jewish population, and being further assured that it will be the policy of the League of Nations to recognize Palestine as a Jewish state as soon as it is a Jewish state in fact.

In harmony with this position, President Woodrow Wilson on March 3, 1919 declared:

I am persuaded that the Allied Nations with the fullest concurrence of our own Government and people are agreed that in Palestine shall be laid the foundations of a Jewish commonwealth.

In the course of recent years, this policy was repeatedly endorsed by numerous Members of Congress, notably in a petition addressed to the President of the United States on November 2, 1943, by 70 Members of the Senate and 194 Members of the House of Representatives, and, on July 2, 1945, by 45 Members of the Senate and 251 Members of the House of Representatives, as well as by the governors of 37 States.

This policy was also endorsed by the national conventions of the Democratic and Republican parties meeting in Chicago in 1944.

It also received the personal endorsement of the late President Roosevelt on October 15, 1944, and, during the same week, of the Republican presidential candidate, Mr. Dewey.

Passage of this resolution will also furnish the occasion for the Congress to express itself forthrightly on the horrible plight of the Jews of Europe, 5,700,000 of whom were victims of Hitler and his madmen, according to the indictment presented by the Allied War Crimes Commission. The war is over and the need for a Jewish homeland, where the Jewish survivors of these persecutions can live and breathe as free men and women, and where they can establish a free and democratic commonwealth is greater than ever. Your committee feels, therefore, that the time is at hand when the long-standing pledges to the Jewish people should be fulfilled.

Appendix 10

CONCURRENT RESOLUTION OF THE CONGRESS OF THE UNITED STATES, DECEMBER 19, 1945

79th Congress
1st Session | S. Con. Res. 44

Concurrent Resolution

Whereas the Sixty-seventh Congress of the United States on June 30, 1922, unanimously resolved "That the United States of America favors the establishment in Palestine of a national home for the Jewish people, it being clearly understood that nothing shall be done which may prejudice the civil and religious rights of Christians and all other non-Jewish communities in Palestine, and that the holy places and religious buildings and sites in Palestine shall be adequately protected", and

Whereas the ruthless persecution of the Jewish people in Europe has clearly demonstrated the need for a Jewish homeland as a haven for the large numbers who have become homeless as a result of this persecution; and

Whereas these urgent necessities are evidenced by the President's request for the immediate right of entry into Palestine of one hundred thousand additional Jewish refugees; and

Whereas the influx of Jewish immigration into Palestine is resulting in its improvement in agricultural, financial, hygienic, and general economic conditions; and

Whereas the President and the British Prime Minister have agreed upon the appointment of a "Joint Anglo-American Committee

* U.S. Statutes at Large, vol. 59, pp. 848-849.

of Enquiry" to examine conditions in Palestine as they bear upon the problem of Jewish immigration and the Jewish situation in Europe and have requested a report within one hundred and twenty days:

Therefore Be It

Resolved by the Senate (the House of Representatives concurring),

That the interest shown by the President in the solution of this problem is hereby commended and that the United States shall use its good offices with the mandatory power to the end that Palestine shall be opened for free entry of Jews into that country to the maximum of its agricultural and economic potentialities, and that there shall be full opportunity for colonization and development, so that they may freely proceed with the upbuilding of Palestine as the Jewish national home and, in association with all elements of the population, establish Palestine as a democratic commonwealth in which all men, regardless of race or creed, shall have equal rights.

Passed the Senate December 17 (legislative day, October 29), 1945.

Attest:

LESLIE L. BIFFLE
Secretary

Notes

(1) The foregoing Resolution likewise passed the House of Representatives on December 19, 1945, as H.Con.Res. 113.

(2) Following is the report of the Committee on Foreign Relations of the United States Senate on the foregoing Resolution:

79th Congress } SENATE { Report
1st Session } { No. 855

Restoration of Palestine as a Homeland
for the Jewish People

December 12 (legislative day, October 29), 1945

—Ordered to be printed

Appendix 11

DECLARATIONS BY PRESIDENTS OF THE UNITED STATES ON PALESTINE AND THE JEWISH NATIONAL HOME

President John Adams (October 1818)*

"I really wish the Jews again in Judaea, an independent Nation, for, as I believe, the most enlightened men of it have participated in the amelioration of the philosophy of the age; once restored to an independent government, and no longer persecuted, they would soon wear away some of the asperities and peculiarities of their character. I wish your nation may be admitted to all the privileges of nations in every part of the world. This country (America) has done much; I wish it may do more, and annul every narrow idea in religion, government and commerce."

President Woodrow Wilson (March 1919)

"As for your representations touching Palestine, I have before this expressed my personal approval of the declaration of the British Government regarding the aspirations and historic claims of the Jewish people in regard to Palestine. I am, moreover, persuaded that the Allied Nations, with the fullest concurrence of our own Government and people, are agreed that in Palestine shall be laid the foundations of a Jewish Commonwealth."

President Calvin Coolidge (June 1924)

"I have so many times reiterated my interest in this great movement that anything which I might add would be a repetition of former

* From discourse on the Restoration of the Jews delivered at the Tabernacle (Congregation) Kabal Kadosh Shearith Israel (The Holy Congregation of the Remnants of Israel) New York City on October 28 and December 2, 1844 by Mordecai Manuel Noah.

statements, but I am nevertheless glad to have this opportunity to express again my sympathy with the deep and intense longing which finds such fine expression in the Jewish National Homeland in Palestine.

"The proposed plan furnishes to the Jewish people an opportunity to devote their great qualities to the upbuilding and preservation of their own homeland and in their own sphere, and I feel sure that the people of the United States will not fail to give that earnest and substantial aid which will be necessary if it is to meet with a full measure of success."

President Herbert Hoover (September 1928):

"I have watched with genuine admiration the steady and unmistakable progress made in the rehabilitation of Palestine which, desolate for centuries, is now renewing its youth and vitality through the enthusiasm, hard work, and self-sacrifice of the Jewish pioneers who toil there in a spirit of peace and social justice. It is very gratifying to note that many American Jews, Zionists as well as non-Zionists, have rendered such splendid service to this cause which merits the sympathy and moral encouragement of everyone."

President Franklin D. Roosevelt (July 1936):

"The interest which I have had and have frequently manifested in the rebuilding of the ancient Jewish homeland is, I am persuaded, an interest which is shared by all who recognize that every people has the inalienable right to life, liberty and the pursuit of happiness. It is a source of renewed hope and courage, that by international accord and by the moral support of the peoples of the world, men and women of Jewish faith have a right to resettle the land where their faith was born and from which much of our modern civilization has emanated."

President Franklin D. Roosevelt (September 1941)

"Efforts will be made to find appropriate ways and means of effectuating this policy as soon as practicable. I know how long and ardently the Jewish people have worked and prayed for the establishment of Palestine as a free and democratic Jewish commonwealth.

I am convinced that the American people give their support to this aim and if re-elected I shall help to bring about its realization."

President Harry S. Truman (October 28, 1946; Letter to the King of Saudi Arabia):

"The Government and the people of the United States have given support to the concept of a Jewish national home in Palestine ever since the termination of the first World War, which resulted in the freeing of a large area of the Near East, including Palestine, and the establishment of a number of independent states which are now members of the United Nations. The United States, which contributed its blood and resources to the winning of that war, could not divest itself of a certain responsibility for the manner in which the freed territories were disposed of, or for the fate of the peoples liberated at that time. It took the position, to which it still adheres, that these peoples should be prepared for self-government and also that a national home for the Jewish people should be established in Palestine. I am happy to note that most of the liberated peoples are now citizens of independent countries. The Jewish national home, however, has not as yet been fully developed.

"It is only natural, therefore, that this Government should favor at this time the entry into Palestine of considerable numbers of displaced Jews in Europe, not only that they may find shelter there but also that they may contribute their talents and energies to the upbuilding of the Jewish national home."

Appendix 12

MAJORITY PLAN OF PARTITION WITH ECONOMIC UNION PROPOSED BY THE UNITED NATIONS SPECIAL COMMITTEE ON PALESTINE AND PASSED BY THE U.N. GENERAL ASSEMBLY ON 29 NOVEMBER, 1947, BY OVER TWO-THIRDS' MAJORITY

1. The basic premise underlying the partition proposal is that the claims to Palestine of the Arabs and Jews, both possessing validity, are irreconcilable, and that among all of the solutions advanced, partition will provide the most realistic and practicable settlement, and is the most likely to afford a workable basis for meeting in part the claims and national aspirations of both parties.

2. It is a fact that both of these peoples have their historic roots in Palestine, and that both make vital contributions to the economic and cultural life of the country. The partition solution takes these considerations fully into account.

3. The basic conflict in Palestine is a clash of two intense nationalisms. Regardless of the historical origins of the conflict, the rights and wrongs of the promises and counter-promises, and the international intervention incident to the Mandate, there are now in Palestine some 650,000 Jews and some 1,200,000 Arabs who are dissimilar in their ways of living and, for the time being, separated by political interests which render difficult full and effective political cooperation among them, whether voluntary or induced by constitutional arrangements.

4. Only by means of partition can these conflicting national aspirations find substantial expression and qualify both peoples to take

their places as independent nations in the international community in the United Nations.

5. The partition solution provides that finality which is a most urgent need in the solution. Every other proposed solution would tend to induce the two parties to seek modification in their favour by means of persistent pressure. The grant of independence to both States, however, would remove the basis for such efforts.

6. Partition is based on a realistic appraisal of the actual Arab-Jewish relations in Palestine. Full political co-operation would be indispensable to the effective functioning of any single-State scheme, such as the federal-State proposal, except in those cases which frankly envisage either an Arab or a Jewish dominated State.

7. Partition is the only means available by which political and economic responsibility can be placed squarely on both Arabs and Jews, with the prospective result that, confronted with the responsibility for bearing fully the consequences of their own actions, a new and important element of political amelioration would be introduced. In the proposed federal-State solution, this factor would be lacking.

8. Jewish immigration is the central issue in Palestine today and is the one factor, above all others, that rules out the necessary co-operation between the Arab and Jewish communities in a single State. The creation of a Jewish State under a partition scheme is the only hope of removing this issue from the arena of conflict.

9. It is recognized that partition has been strongly opposed by Arabs, but it is felt that the opposition would be lessened by a solution which definitively fixes the extent of territory to be allotted to the Jews with its implicit limitation on immigration. The fact that the solution carries the sanction of the United Nations involves a finality which should allay Arab fears of further expansion of the Jewish State.

10. In view of the limited area and resources of Palestine, it is essential that, to the extent feasible, and consistent with the

creation of two independent States, the economic unity of the country should be preserved. The partition proposal, therefore, is a qualified partition, subject to such measures and limitations as are considered essential to the future economic and social well-being of both States. Since the economic self-interest of each State would be vitally involved, it is believed that the minimum measure of economic unity is possible, where that of political unity is not.

11. Such economic unity requires the creation of an economic association by means of a treaty between the two States. The essential objectives of this association would be a common customs system, a common currency and the maintenance of a country-wide system of transport and communications.

12. The maintenance of existing standards of social services in all parts of Palestine depends partly upon the preservation of economic unity, and this is a main consideration underlying the provisions for an economic union as part of the partition scheme. Partition, however, necessarily changes to some extent the fiscal situation in such a manner that, at any rate during the early years of its existence, a partitioned Arab State in Palestine would have some difficulty in raising sufficient revenues to keep up its present standards of public services.

One of the aims of the economic union, therefore, is to distribute surplus revenue to support such standards. It is recommended that the division of the surplus revenue, after certain charges and percentage of surplus to be paid to the City of Jerusalem are met, should be in equal proportions to the two States. This is an arbitrary proportion but it is considered that it would be acceptable, that it has the merit of simplicity and that, being fixed in this manner, it would be less likely to become a matter of controversy. Provisions are suggested whereby this formula is to be reviewed.

13. This division of customs revenue is justified on three grounds: (1) The Jews will have the more economically developed part of the country embracing practically the whole of the citrus-producing area which includes a large number of Arab producers; (2) the Jewish State would, through the customs union, be guaranteed a larger free trade area for the sale of the products

of its industry; (3) it would be to the disadvantage of the Jewish State if the Arab State should be in a financially precarious and poor economic condition.

14. As the Arab State will not be in a position to undertake considerable development expenditure, sympathetic consideration should be given to its claims for assistance from international institutions in the way of loans for expansion of education, public health and other vital social services of a non-self-supporting nature.

15. International financial assistance would also be required for any comprehensive irrigation schemes in the interest of both States, and it is to be hoped that constructive work by the Joint Economic Board will be made possible by means of international loans on favourable terms.

* UN Doc. A/364, 3 September 1947.

** UN Official Records of the Second Session of the General Assembly, Resolutions (16 September-29 November 1947), pp. 131-150.

APPENDIX 13

DECLARATION OF THE ESTABLISHMENT OF THE STATE OF ISRAEL*

ERETZ ISRAEL[1] was the birthplace of the Jewish people. Here their spiritual, religious and political identity was shaped. Here they first attained to statehood, created cultural values of national and universal significance and gave to the world the eternal Book of Books.

After being forcibly exiled from their land, the people kept faith with it throughout their Dispersion and never ceased to pray and hope for their return to it and for the restoration in it of their political freedom.

Impelled by this historic and traditional attachment, Jews strove in every successive generation to re-establish themselves in their ancient homeland. In recent decades they returned in their masses. Pioneers, *ma'pilim*[2] and defenders, they made deserts bloom, revived the Hebrew language, built villages and towns, and created a thriving community, controlling its own economy and culture, loving peace but knowing how to defend itself, bringing the blessings of progress to all the country's inhabitants, and aspiring towards independent nationhood.

In the year 5657 (1897), at the summons of the spiritual father of the Jewish State, Theodor Herzl, the First Zionist Congress convened and proclaimed the right of the Jewish people to national rebirth in its own country.

This right was recognized in the Balfour Declaration of the 2nd November, 1917, and re-affirmed in the Mandate of the League of

* Published in the *Official Gazette,* No. 1 of the 5th Iyar, 5708 (14th May, 1948).
1 *Eretz-Israel* (Hebrew) — the Land of Israel, Palestine.
2 *Ma'pilim* (Hebrew) — immigrants coming to Eretz-Israel in defiance of restrictive legislation.

Nations which, in particular, gave international sanction to the historic connection between the Jewish people and Eretz-Israel and to the right of the Jewish people to rebuild its National Home.

The catastrophe which recently befell the Jewish people—the massacre of millions of Jews in Europe—was another clear demonstration of the urgency of solving the problem of its homelessness by re-establishing in Eretz-Israel the Jewish State, which would open the gates of the homeland wide to every Jew and confer upon the Jewish people the status of a fully-privileged member of the comity of nations.

Survivors of the Nazi holocaust in Europe, as well as Jews from other parts of the world, continued to migrate to Eretz-Israel, undaunted by difficulties, restrictions and dangers, and never ceased to assert their right to a life of dignity, freedom and honest toil in their national homeland.

In the Second World War, the Jewish community of this country contributed its full share to the struggle of the freedom- and peace-loving nations against the forces of Nazi wickedness and, by the blood of its soldiers and its war effort, gained the right to be reckoned among the peoples who founded the United Nations.

On the 29th November, 1947, the United Nations General Assembly passed a resolution calling for the establishment of a Jewish State in Eretz-Israel; the General Assembly required the inhabitants of Eretz-Israel to take such steps as were necessary on their part for the implementation of that resolution. This recognition by the United Nations of the right of the Jewish people to establish their State is irrevocable.

This right is the natural right of the Jewish people to be masters of their own fate, like all other nations, in their own sovereign State.

ACCORDINGLY WE, MEMBERS OF THE PEOPLE'S COUNCIL, REPRESENTATIVES OF THE JEWISH COMMUNITY OF ERETZ-ISRAEL AND OF THE ZIONIST MOVEMENT, ARE HERE ASSEMBLED ON THE DAY OF THE TERMINATION OF THE BRITISH MANDATE OVER ERETZ-ISRAEL AND, BY VIRTUE OF OUR NATURAL AND HISTORIC RIGHT AND ON THE STRENGTH OF THE RESOLUTION OF THE UNITED NATIONS GENERAL ASSEMBLY, HEREBY DECLARE THE ESTABLISHMENT OF A JEWISH STATE IN ERETZ-ISRAEL, TO BE KNOWN AS THE STATE OF ISRAEL.

WE DECLARE that, with effect from the moment of the termination of the Mandate, being tonight, the eve of Sabbath, the 6th Iyar, 5708 (15th May, 1948), until the establishment of the elected, regular authorities of the State in accordance with the Constitution which shall be adopted by the Elected Constituent Assembly not later than the 1st October, 1948, the People's Council shall act as a Provisional Council of State, and its executive organ, the People's Administration, shall be the Provisional Government of the Jewish State, to be called "Israel".

THE STATE OF ISRAEL will be open for Jewish immigration and for the ingathering of the exiles; it will foster the development of the country for the benefit of all inhabitants; it will be based on freedom, justice and peace as envisaged by the prophets of Israel; it will ensure complete equality of social and political rights to all its inhabitants irrespective of religion, race or sex; it will guarantee freedom of religion, conscience, language, education and culture; it will safeguard the Holy Places of all religions; and it will be faithful to the principles of the Charter of the United Nations.

THE STATE OF ISRAEL is prepared to cooperate with the agencies and representatives of the United Nations in implementing the resolution of the General Assembly of the 29th November, 1947, and will take steps to bring about the economic union of the whole of Eretz-Israel.

WE APPEAL to the United Nations to assist the Jewish people in the building-up of its State and to receive the State of Israel into the comity of nations.

WE APPEAL—in the very midst of the onslaught launched against us now for months—to the Arab inhabitants of the State of Israel to preserve peace and participate in the upbuilding of the State on the basis of full and equal citizenship and due representation in all its provisional and permanent institutions.

WE EXTEND our hand to all neighbouring States and their peoples in an offer of peace and good neighborliness, and appeal to them to establish bonds of cooperation and mutual help with the sovereign Jewish people settled in its own land. The State of Israel is prepared to do its share in common effort for the advancement of the entire Middle East.

WE APPEAL to the Jewish people throughout the Diaspora to rally round the Jews of Eretz-Israel in the tasks of immigration and upbuilding and to stand by them in the great struggle for the realization of the age-old dream—the redemption of Israel.

PLACING OUR TRUST IN THE ALMIGHTY, WE AFFIX OUR SIGNATURES TO THIS PROCLAMATION AT THIS SESSION OF THE PROVISIONAL COUNCIL OF STATE, ON THE SOIL OF THE HOMELAND, IN THE CITY OF TEL AVIV, ON THIS SABBATH EVE, THE 5th DAY OF IYAR, 5708 (14th MAY, 1948).

David Ben-Gurion

Daniel Auster
Mordekhai Bentov
Yitzchak Ben Zvi
Eliyahu Berligne
Fritz Bernstein
Rabbi Wolf Gold
Meïr Grabovsky
Yitzchak Gruenbaum
Dr. Abraham Granovsky
Eliyahu Dobkin
Meir Wilner-Kovner
Zerach Wahrhaftig
Herzl Vardi
Rachel Cohen
Rabbi Kalman Kahana
Saadia Kobashi
Rabbi Yitzchak Meir Levin
Meir David Loevenstein
Zvi Luria
Golda Myerson
Nachum Nir
Zvi Segal
Rabbi Yehuda Leib Hacohen Fishman
David Zvi Pinkas
Aharon Zisling
Moshe Kolodny
Eliezer Kaplan
Abraham Katznelson
Felix Rosenblueth
David Remez
Berl Repetur
Mordekhai Shattner
Ben Zion Sternberg
Bekhor Shitreet
Moshe Shapira
Moshe Shertok

APPENDIX 14

ISRAEL-ARAB ARMISTICE AGREEMENTS—1949

{The following extracts from the Israel-Jordan Armistice Agreement, signed under United Nations auspices at Rhodes, April 13, 1949, are identical in letter and spirit with the Armistice Agreements signed by Israel and Egypt, Israel and Syria and Israel and Lebanon.}

Security Council Document S/1302/Rev.1

Cablegram dated 3 April 1949 from the United Nations Acting Mediator to the Secretary-General transmitting the text of the General Armistice Agreement between the Hashemite Jordan Kingdom and Israel.

(Original text: English)
Rhodes, 3 April 1949

For the President of the Security Council

I have the honour to inform you that an armistice agreement between the Hashemite Jordan Kingdom and Israel has been signed this evening, 3 April 1949, at Rhodes. The text of the agreement follows.

RALPH J. BUNCHE
Acting Mediator

Hashemite Jordan Kingdom — Israel
General Armistice Agreement

Rhodes, 3 April 1949

Preamble

The Parties to the present Agreement,

Responding to the Security Council resolution of 16 November 1948, calling upon them, as a further provisional measure under Article 40 of the Charter of the United Nations and in order to facilitate the transition from the present truce to permanent peace in Palestine, to negotiate an armistice;

Having decided to enter into negotiations under United Nations chairmanship concerning the implementation of the Security Council resolution of 16 November 1948; and having appointed representatives empowered to negotiate and conclude an Armistice Agreement,

The undersigned representatives of their respective Governments, having exchanged their full powers found to be in good and proper form, have agreed upon the following provisions:

Article I

With a view to promoting the return of permanent peace in Palestine and in recognition of the importance in this regard of mutual assurances concerning the future military operations of the Parties, the following principles, which shall be fully observed by both Parties during the armistice, are hereby affirmed:

1. The injunction of the Security Council against resort to military force in the settlement of the Palestine question shall henceforth be scrupulously respected by both Parties;

2. No aggressive action by the armed forces—land, sea or air—of either Party shall be undertaken, planned, or threatened against the people or the armed forces of the other; it being understood that the use of the term "planned" in this context has no bearing on normal staff planning as generally practised in military organization;

3. The right of each Party to its security and freedom from fear of attack by the armed forces of the other shall be fully respected;

4. The establishment of an armistice between the armed forces of the two Parties is accepted as an indispensable step toward the liquidation of armed conflict and the restoration of peace in Palestine.

Article III

1. In pursuance of the foregoing principles and of the resolution of the Security Council of 16 November 1948, a general armistice between the armed forces of the two Parties—land, sea and air—is hereby established.

2. No element of the land, sea or air, military or para-military forces of either Party, including non-regular forces, shall commit any warlike or hostile act against the military or para-military forces of

the other Party, or against civilians in territory under the control of that Party; or shall advance beyond or pass over for any purpose whatsoever the Armistice Demarcation Lines set forth in articles V and VI of this Agreement; or enter into or pass through the air space of the other Party.

3. No warlike act or act of hostility shall be conducted from territory controlled by one of the Parties to this Agreement against the other Party.

{The following article No. 8, is specific to the Israel-Jordan Armistice Agreement, as it deals with the agreement between the two countries providing for free access to Mt. Scopus, holy places and cultural institutions, use of the cemetery on the Mount of Olives, and other matters connected with the Jerusalem area.}

Article VIII

1. A Special Committee, composed of two representatives of each Party designated by the respective Governments, shall be established for the purpose of formulating agreed plans and arrangements designed to enlarge the scope of this Agreement and to effect improvements in its application.

2. The Special Committee shall be organized immediately following the coming into effect of this Agreement and shall direct its attention to the formulation of agreed plans and arrangements for such matters as either Party may submit to it, which, in any case, shall include the following, on which agreement in principle already exists: free movement of traffic on vital roads, including the Bethlehem and Latrun-Jerusalem roads; resumption of the normal functioning of the cultural and humanitarian institutions on Mount Scopus and free access thereto; free access to the Holy Places and cultural institutions and use of the cemetery on the Mount of Olives; resumption of operation of the Latrun pumping station; provision of electricity for the Old City; and resumption of operation of the railroad to Jerusalem.

3. The Special Committee shall have exclusive competence over such matters as may be referred to it. Agreed plans and arrangements fomulated by it may provide for the exercise of supervisory functions by the Mixted Armistice Commission established in article XI.

Article XI

1. The execution of the provisions of this Agreement, with the exception of such matters as fall within the exclusive competence of the Special Committee established in article VIII, shall be supervised by a Mixed Armistice Commission composed of five members, of whom each Party to this Agreement shall designate two, and whose Chairman shall be the United Nations Chief of Staff of the Truce Supervision Organization or a senior officer from the observer personnel of that organization designated by him following consultation with both Parties to this Agreement.

2. The Mixed Armistice Commission shall maintain its headquarters at Jerusalem and shall hold its meetings at such places and at such times as it may deem necessary for the effective conduct of its work.

3. The Mixed Armistice Commission shall be convened in its first meeting by the United Nations Chief of Staff of the Truce Supervision Organization and not later than one week following the signing of this Agreement.

4. Decisions of the Mixed Armistice Commission, to the extent possible, shall be based on the principle of unanimity. In the absence of unanimity, decisions shall be taken by a majority vote of the members of the Commission present and voting.

5. The Mixed Armistice Commission shall formulate its own rules of procedure. Meetings shall be held only after due notice to the members by the Chairman. The quorum for its meetings shall be a majority of its members.

6. The Commission shall be empowered to employ observers, who may be from among the military organizations of the Parties or from the military personnel of the United Nations Truce Supervision Organization, or from both, in such numbers as may be considered essential to the performance of its functions. In the event United Nations observers should be so employed, they shall remain under the command of the United Nations Chief of Staff of the Truce Supervision Organization. Assignments of a general or special nature given to United Nations observers attached to the Mixed Armistice Commission shall be subject to approval by the United Nations Chief of Staff or his designated representative on the Commission, whichever is serving as Chairman.

7. Claims or complaints presented by either Party relating to the application of this Agreement shall be referred immediately to the Mixed Armistice Commission through its Chairman. The Commission shall take such action on all such claims or complaints by means of its observation and investigation machinery as it may deem appropriate, with a view to equitable and mutually satisfactory settlement.

8. Where interpretation of the meaning of a particular provision of this Agreement, other than the preamble and articles I and II, is at issue, the Commission's interpretation shall prevail. The Commission, in its discretion and as the need arises, may from time to time recommend to the Parties modifications in the provisions of this Agreement.

9. The Mixed Armistice Commission shall submit to both Parties reports on its activities as frequently as it may consider necessary. A copy of each such report shall be presented to the Secretary-General of the United Nations for transmission to the appropriate organ or agency of the United Nations.

10. Members of the Commission and its observers shall be accorded such freedom of movement and access in the area covered by this Agreement as the Commission may determine to be necessary, provided that when such decisions of the Commission are reached by a majority vote United Nations observers only shall be employed.

11. The expenses of the Commission, other than those relating to United Nations observers, shall be apportioned in equal shares between the two Parties to this Agreement.

{Article XII of this Agreement stipulates that the Parties may call upon the UN Secretary-General to convoke a conference of the representatives for the purpose of reviewing, revising or suspending any of its provisions other than articles I and III.}

Article XII

1. The present Agreement is not subject to ratification and shall come into force immediately upon being signed.

2. This Agreement, having been negotiated and concluded in pursuance of the resolution of the Security Council of 16 November 1948 calling for the establishment of an armistice in order to eliminate the threat to peace in Palestine and to facilitate the transition from the

present truce to permanent peace in Palestine, shall remain in force until a peaceful settlement between the Parties is achieved, except as provided in paragraph 3 of this article.

3. The Parties to this Agreement may, by mutual consent, revise this Agreement or any of its provisions, or may suspend its application, other than articles I and III, at any time. In the absence of mutual agreement and after this Agreement has been in effect for one year from the date of its signing, either of the Parties may call upon the Secretary-General of the United Nations to convoke a conference of representatives of the two Parties for the purpose of reviewing, revising, or suspending any of the provisions of this Agreement other than articles I and III. Participation in such conference shall be obligatory upon the Parties.

4. If the conference provided for in paragraph 3 of this article does not result in an agreed solution of a point in dispute, either Party may bring the matter before the Security Council of the United Nations for the relief sought on the grounds that this Agreement has been concluded in pursuance of Security Council action toward the end of achieving peace in Palestine.

5. This Agreement is signed in quintuplicate, of which one copy shall be retained by each Party, two copies communicated to the Secretary-General of the United Nations for transmission to the Security Council and to the United Nations Conciliation Commission on Palestine, and one copy to the United Nations Acting Mediator on Palestine.

DONE at Rhodes, Island of Rhodes, Greece, on the third of April one thousand nine hundred and forty-nine in the presence of the United Nations Acting Mediator on Palestine and the United Nations Chief of Staff of the Truce Supervision Organization.

For and on behalf of the Government of the Hashemite Jordan Kingdom	For and on behalf of the Government of Israel
(signed)	(signed)
COLONEL AHMED SUDKI EL-JUNDI	REUVEN SHILOAH
LIEUTENANT-COLONEL MOHAMED MAAYTE	LIEUTENANT-COLONEL MOSHE DAYAN

Appendix 15

FREEDOM OF PASSAGE THROUGH SUEZ CANAL

(Relevant Operative Paragraphs of Constantinople Convention of 1888, decisions of UN Security Council 1951 and 1956 and Egyptian declaration of acceptance of ruling of UN Security Council.)

Constantinople Convention, 1888

Articles I and IV of the Treaty of Constantinople establish the principle of freedom of passage.

Article I provides:

"The Suez Maritime Canal shall always be free and open, in time of war as in time of peace, to every vessel of commerce or of war, without distinction of flag.

"Consequently, the High Contracting Parties agree not in any way to interfere with the free use of the Canal, in time of war as in time of peace.

"The Canal shall never be subjected to the exercise of the rights of blockade."

The first paragraph of article IV declares:

"The Maritime Canal remaining open in time of war as a free passage, even to ships of war of belligerents, according to the terms of Article I of the present Treaty, the High Contracting Parties agree that no right of war, no act of hostility, nor any act having for its object to obstruct the free navigation of the Canal, shall be committed in the Canal and its ports of access, as well as within a radius of three marine miles from those ports, even though the Ottoman Empire should be one of the belligerent Powers."

Article X:

"Similarly, the provisions of Articles IV, V, VII and VIII shall not interfere with the measures which His Majesty the Sultan and His Highness the Khedive, in the name of His Imperial Majesty, and within the limits of the Firmans granted, might find it necessary to take for securing by their own forces the defence of Egypt and the maintenance of public order.

"In case His Imperial Majesty the Sultan, or His Highness the Khedive, should find it necessary to avail themselves of the exceptions for which this article provides, the Signatory Powers of the Declaration of London shall be notified thereof by the Imperial Ottoman Government.

"It is likewise understood that the provisions of the four Articles aforesaid shall in no case occasion any obstacle to the measures which the Imperial Ottoman Government may think it necessary to take in order to insure by its own forces the defence of its other possessions situated on the eastern coast of the Red Sea."

Article XI:

"The measures which shall be taken in the cases provided for by Articles IX and X of the present Treaty shall not interfere with the free use of the Canal. In the same cases, the erection of permanent fortifications contrary to the provisions of Article VIII is prohibited."

Article XIV:

"The High Contracting Parties agree that the engagements resulting from the present Treaty shall not be limited by the duration of the Acts of Concession of the Universal Suez Canal Company."

UN Security Council Resolutions

The Council's Resolution of I September 1951 affirms:

"that since the Armistice (Israel-Egypt Armistice Agreement 1949) regime which has been in existence for nearly two and a half years is of a permanent character, neither party can reasonably assert that it is actively a belligerent or requires to exercise the right of visit, search, and seizure for any legitimate purpose of self-defence." (Paragraph 5) "that practice cannot in the prevailing circumstances be justified on the grounds that it is necessary for self-defence." (Paragraph 8)

"The restrictions on the passage of goods through the Suez Canal to Israeli ports are denying to nations at no time connected with conflict in Palestine valuable supplies required for their economic reconstruction, and . . . these restrictions together with sanctions applied by Egypt to certain ships which have visited Israeli ports represent unjustified interference with the rights of nations to navigate the seas and to trade freely with one another, including the Arab States and Israel." (Paragraph 9)

"Calls upon Egypt to terminate the restrictions on the passage of international commercial shipping and goods through the Suez Canal wherever bound and to cease all interference with such shipping beyond that essential to the safety of shipping in the Canal itself and to the observance of the international conventions in force."

The Council's Resolution of 13 October 1956—of six principles unanimously adopted to govern free international navigation, the following are the two principal ones:

"(1) There should be free and open transit through the Canal without discrimination, overt or covert—this covers both political and technical aspects."

"(3) The operation of the Canal should be insulated from the politics of any country."

Declaration by the Egyptian Government to the Secretary-General of the United Nations on 24 April 1957 (registered as an International Treaty under Article 102 of the Charter (S/3818):

"It remains the unaltered policy and firm purpose of the Government of Egypt to respect the terms and the spirit of the Constantinople Convention of 1888 and the rights and obligations arising therefrom. The Government of Egypt will continue to respect, observe and implement them.

"The Government of Egypt are more particularly determined:

a. To afford and maintain free and uninterrupted navigation for all nations within the limits of and in accordance with the provisions of the Constantinople Convention of 1888.

The representative of Egypt stated at the Security Council meeting of 20 May 1957 (S/PV 778):

"The Declaration is in keeping with that Resolution (i.e. of 13 October 1956) and hence with the six principles, and even with the most difficult of them, the 3rd, which states that the operation of the Canal shall be insulated from the politics of any country."

Appendix 16

سري جداً

الفرقة الثالثة المشاة
(العمليات)
رقم القيد [illegible]
التاريخ ٢٥ مايو ٥٦

الموضوع توجيهات قا فر ٣ مش رقم (١)

قائد القتال المصري بفلسطين

قائد مجموعة اللواء السادس المشاة

الآتي بعد موجز توجيهات قائد الفرقة الثالثة المشاة للضباط في الأيام والتواريخ الموجه بعد :-

المجدل	يوم ١ سبتمبر ٥٦
[illegible]	" ٣ " "
خان يونس	" [illegible] " "
[illegible]	" [illegible] " "

[illegible] من جميع الضباط مع ملاحظة ألا تنشر هذه التوجيهات كتابة [illegible]
[illegible] من الوحدات الأخرى

أ - مقدمة

على كل قائد أن يعد نفسه ورجاله لخوض غمار المعركة [illegible] مع إسرائيل [illegible]
لتحقيق هدفنا الأسمى وهو القضاء على إسرائيل وإبادتها بأقصر وقت وبأقسى صوره الوحشيه
في القتال .

ب - التدريب

أ - التدريب [illegible] لا يمكن [illegible]
ب - يجب أن [illegible] في القتال [illegible]
ج - يجب أن [illegible]
(١) [illegible] في القتال [illegible]
(٢) [illegible]
[illegible]
(٣) [illegible] في جميع [illegible] .

ج - [illegible]

أ - لا [illegible] على الضباط [illegible] من جميع [illegible]
ب - يجب أن [illegible] على [illegible]
[illegible] ..
(١) [illegible]
(٢) [illegible]
(٣) [illegible]
(٤) [illegible]
(٥) [illegible] .

د - الشخصية [illegible]

(١) يجب أن [illegible]
[illegible]
(٢) يجب أن [illegible]

[illegible]

يجب ... [illegible]

وهذا ... [illegible]

[illegible]

هـ - ولهذا يجب أن يشمل التكوين ... [illegible]

(١) [illegible]

(٢) [illegible]

(٣) [illegible]

[illegible]

[illegible]

- الأسلحة والمعدات

يجب أن يمتلك القادة على كافة المستويات ما يلي :-

[illegible]

- المواصلات

يجب أن [illegible]

- الإسعافات

[illegible]

- التدريب

[illegible]

[illegible]

APPENDIX 16 (Translation)

{Translation of preceding document dated Feb. 15, 1956 captured in Gaza showing Egyptian preparations for offensive against Israel. This document is one of many of a similar nature captured.}

Top Secret

3rd Infantry Division (Operations)   Subject: Directive No 2 of Commander 3rd Infantry Division

Registration No. 558/2/56/2/5/E

Date: 15 February 1956

(From) C.O. Egyptian District, Palestine

(To) C.O. Reinforced 5th Infantry Brigade

The following is the essence of the Directives of the Commander of the 3rd Division to commanders and officers on the days and dates listed below:

El Arish	Day	1 Feb. 56
Rafah	Day	3 Feb. 56
Khan Yunis	Day	4 Feb. 56
Gaza	Day	4 Feb. 56

Please see to the execution of these Directives by all officers and ensure that These Directives shall not be put down in writing for classification lower than battalion or parallel classification in other units.

(1) INTRODUCTION

Every commander must prepare himself and his soldiers for the important battle with Israel in which we are fully immersed, with the aim of realizing our lofty tradition, i.e., to overpower and destroy Israel in the shortest possible time and with the greatest brutality and bestiality in battle.

(2) TRAINING

a. Training is the basic factor in the attainment of our goal. Without it, it is impossible to achieve victory.

b. Our faith in battle must be in all ranks, a faith in aggressiveness and speed.

c. The following factors must be part of the training:
   1) Perserverance and strong will to fight brutally.
   2) Training in leading men and their commanding officers gaining their confidence and affection. Any breach of discipline by soldiers against their officers must be prevented.
   3) Earnestness and realism in all our actions.

(3) The COMMANDERS

a. The term Commander is not limited to an officer but applies to anyone of any rank who has to give commands.

b. Our policy must be built up on the preparation of commanders for the next ten years. Aid to prepare commanders and their units . . .
   1) High discipline.
   2) Knowledge, and the increase of knowledge.
   3) Absolute obedience and loyalty to commander.
   4) Tact, initiative and care of equipment.
   5) Good example in leading men: treating men in order to gain their confidence and affection.

c. Personality of Commander:
   1) The commander should control his men more by personal example than by punishment.
   2) He must accept every decision of his superior officer without hesitation.
   3) When the commander imposes his personality on his unit, hesitations about entering battle are dispelled, regardless of reasons such as lack of time or equipment. His personality is thus decisive in determining the victorious outcome of the battle.

d. Hence the annual report of officers in general and commanders in particular must include:—
   1) The level of ability of the commander.
   2) His ability to lead his men.
   3) His ability to take care of his equipment.

e. The mistakes made by the commander when he takes fateful decisions or when he executes an order given to him, are not to be condemned, because they teach a lesson that must be put to use.

Mistakes emanating from carelessness, however, including those from unfitting behaviour, should be treated with all severity.

f. Clarity in giving orders, the exposure of errors, the expression of opinions and criticism, are the right and duty of every commander. Forthrightness must be a constructive, and not a destructive factor. It must not be an instrument of degradation. Implied by this is also appreciation of diligence and fitting and constructive guidance of the one who errs.

g. Commanders of all rank must understand that their place is not in offices but rather with their soldiers, either training, directing or educating them, studying their social problems and participating with them in sport and entertainment.

(4) Arms and equipment.

Commanders of all ranks must make certain that:—

a. Every weapon shall be fit for action and efficient use by periodic tests with live ammunition.

b. That vehicles are fit for service. Drivers must be instructed in their proper maintenance. They must be given instructions against over-speeding.

(5) Fortifications.

Trenches should be examined to ensure that they are as deep as a man's requirements. Arms must be examined in the light of ability to use them from this position, and with the view of testing the soldier's expertness in aiming and fire.

(6) Inspection

It is expected that a number of commanders of units of the Central District will conduct a tour of inspection in the area of the unit. We must therefore be worthy of appreciation and be able to explain the situation, whether by means of maps or on the ground, each according to his level. Likewise, it is possible that a number of officers and other ranks of the unit will conduct tours of inspection of the battle order of the units of the Central District, within a period of seven hours, beginning and ending in Abu Ageilah.

(7) Hit and Run Policy:

Hit and run policy is transformed into aggressive policy as follows:—

a. 5th Brigade—in constant preparedness.

b. 3rd Brigade should arrive by 1st April 1956 for company assault training within the framework of the battalion.

c. 86th Brigade must arrive by 1st April 1956 for company assault training regardless of present shortage of manpower and equipment.

d. The National Guard must complete the training of its volunteers in invasion tactics, without regard to training received preceding their entry into camp. The training of every course must end within seven weeks from arrival at the camp.

(8) Our aim is always "the destruction of Israel". Remember and act for its attainment.

(—)
Liwa (Major-General) Ahmed Salem
Staff Officer

Appendix 17

BREAKDOWN OF ARAB ATTACKS ON AND OVER ISRAEL'S BORDERS — 1951-1956

{From 1951 to 1956 Arab attacks reached dangerous proportions. After Israel's Sinai operation they ceased.}

	Year	Killed	Wounded	Dynamiting Mining	Armed Clashes	Robbery	Theft and Att. Theft	Border Incursions
Lebanon	1951	1	2	—	9	4	8	—
	1952	1	—	—	8	1	22	—
	1953	2	7	—	16	3	13	—
	1954	—	—	—	8	2	13	—
	1955	2	9	1	6	—	11	19
	Total	6	18	1	47	10	57	20
I-VIII	1956	1	12	4	11	2	5	40
1951- IX of	1956	7	30	5	58	12	62	60
Syria	1951	48	44	1	47	—	12	—
	1952	1	2	—	16	—	13	—
	1953	—	3	—	18	—	5	—
	1954	—	4	—	24	2	8	42
	1955	6	15	1	109	2	2	50
	Total	55	68	2	214	4	40	92
I-VIII	1956	4	4	2	47	1	2	132
1951- IX of	1956	59	72	4	261	5	42	224

	Year	Killed	Wounded	Dynamiting Mining	Armed Clashes	Robbery	Theft and Att. Theft	Border Incursions
Jordan	1949	11	17	34	84	88	—	9
	1950	18	36	37	99	100	—	54
	1951	44	75	31	309	1423	—	210
	1952	46	74	27	320	1154	—	519
	1953	57	80	18	325	722	—	388
	1954	34	92	4	291	229	—	207
	1955	11	36	16	138	169	—	55
	Total	221	410	167	1566	3885	—	1442
I-VIII	1956	36	57	12	157	4	58	102
1949-IX of	1956	257	468	179	1723	3947	—	1544
Egypt	1951	7	11	10	102	2	216	—
	1952	8	21	20	142	8	553	—
	1953	8	18	22	99	11	549	—
	1954	7	43	9	135	13	289	42
	1955	48	144	49	199	8	128	137
	Total	78	237	110	677	42	1715	179
I-VIII	1956	23	103	62	362	1	85	256
1951-IX of	1956	101	340	172	1039	43	1800	435

Bibliography

HISTORICAL BACKGROUND

Bein, Alexander, *The Return to the Soil: A History of Jewish Settlement in Israel.* Jerusalem, Youth and Hechalutz Department, Zionist Organization, 1952.

Bein, Alexander, *Theodor Herzl: A Biography.* Philadelphia, Jewish Publication Society of America, 1941.

Bilby, Kenneth W., *New Star in the Near East.* New York, Doubleday, 1950.

Book of Documents. New York, Jewish Agency for Palestine, 1947.

Brandeis, Louis D., *Brandeis on Zionism.* New York, Zionist Organization of America, 1942.

Buber, Martin, *Israel and Palestine: The History of an Idea.* New York, Farrar, Straus and Cudahy, 1952.

Cohen, Israel, *The Zionist Movement.* New York, Zionist Organization of America, 1946.

Crum, Bartley C., *Behind the Silken Curtain:* A Personal Account of Anglo-American Diplomacy in Palestine and the Middle East. New York, Simon and Schuster, 1947.

Esco Foundation for Palestine, Inc., *Palestine: A Study of Jewish, Arab and British Policies.* New Haven, Yale University Press, 1947, 2 v.

Fink, Reuben, ed., *America and Palestine.* New York American Zionist Emergency Council, 1944.

Frankenstein, Ernst, *Palestine in the Light of International Law.* New York, 1947.

Garcia-Granados, Jorge, *The Birth of Israel: The Drama As I Saw It.* New York, Knopf, 1948.

Government of Palestine, *Survey of Palestine 1946.* Jerusalem, Government Printer.

Granott, Abraham, *Agrarian Reform and the Record of Israel.* London, Eyre and Spottiswoode, 1956.

Horowitz, David, *State in the Making.* Translated from the Hebrew by Julian Meltzer. New York, Knopf, 1953.

Hull, William Lovell, *The Fall and Rise of Israel:* The Story of the Jewish People During the Time of Their Dispersal and Regathering. Grand Rapids, Zondervan Publishing Co., 1954.

The Jewish Case Before the Anglo-American Committee of Inquiry on Palestine. Jerusalem, Jewish Agency, 1947.

The Jewish Plan for Palestine. Jerusalem, Jewish Agency, 1947.

Joseph, Bernard, *British Rule in Palestine.* Washington, D.C., Public Affairs Press, 1948.

Kimche, Jon and David, *The Secret Roads: The "Illegal" Migration of a People, 1938-1984.* New York, Farrar, Straus and Cudahy, 1955.

Lloyd George, David, *The Truth About the Peace Treaties.* London, 1938.

Lowdermilk, Walter Clay, *Palestine, Land of Promise.* New York, Harper and Bros., 1944.

Miller, Irving, *Israel, the Eternal Ideal.* New York, Farrar, Straus and Cudahy, 1955.

O'Ballance, Edgar, *The Arab-Israeli War 1948.* New York, Praeger, 1957.

Owen, George Frederick, *Abraham to the Middle East Crisis.* 4th ed. rev., Grand Rapids, Eerdmans, 1957.

Palestine Royal Commission Report, London, Government Printer, 1937.

Parkes, James W., *End of an Exile: Israel, the Jews and the Gentile World.* New York, Library Publishers, 1954.

Parkes, James W., *A History of Palestine from 135 A.D. to Modern Times.* New York, Oxford University Press, 1949

Revusky, Abraham, *Jews in Palestine.* New York, Bloch Publishing Co., 1945.

Rosenne, Shabtai, *Israel's Armistice Agreements with the Arab States.* Tel Aviv, 1951.

Royal Institute of International Affairs, *Great Britain and Palestine.* London, Oxford University Press, 1939.

Twain, Mark, *The Innocents Abroad.* Harper and Bros. edition.

Uris, Leon, *Exodus.* New York, Doubleday, 1959.

Weizmann, Chaim, *Trial and Error: The Autobiography of Chaim Weizmann.* Philadelphia, Jewish Publication Society of America, 1949.

ISRAEL

Bachi, Roberto, ed., *Studies in Economic and Social Sciences.* Ed. on behalf of the Eliezer Kaplan School of Economics and Social Sciences, Jerusalem, Magnes Press, Hebrew University, 1956.

Baratz, Joseph, *A Village by the Jordan: The Story of Degania.* New York, Sharon Books, 1957.

Ben-Gurion, David, *Rebirth and Destiny of Israel.* Ed. and tr. from the Hebrew under the supervision of Mordekhai Nurock, New York, Philosophical Library, 1954.

Bentwich, Norman De Mattos, *Israel.* New York, McGraw Hill, 1952.

Bernstein, Marver H., *The Politics of Israel: The First Decade of Statehood.* Princeton, Princeton University Press, 1957.

Davis, Moshe, ed., *Israel: Its Role in Civilization.* New York, Harper and Bros., 1956.

Eban, Abba Solomon, *Voice of Israel.* New York, Horizon Press, 1957.

Eisenstadt, Samuel N., *The Absorption of Immigrants.* Glencoe, Ill., Free Press, 1955.

Elath, Eliahu, *Israel and Her Neighbors:* Lectures Delivered at Brandeis University. Cleveland, World Publishing Co., 1957.

Eytan, Walter, *The First Ten Years: A Diplomatic History of Israel.* New York, Simon and Schuster, 1958.

Frankenstein, Carl, ed., *Between Past and Future:* Essays and Studies on Aspects of Immigrant Absorption in Israel. Jerusalem, Henrietta Szold Foundation for Child and Youth Welfare, 1953.

Grossman, Kurt R., *Germany's Moral Debt: The German-Israel Agreement.* Washington, D.C., Public Affairs Press, 1954.

Halkin, Simon, *Modern Hebrew Literature: Trends and Values.* New York, Schocken Books, 1950.

Halperin, Haim, *Changing Patterns in Israel Agriculture.* London, Routledge and Kegan Paul, 1957.

Henriques, R., *One Hundred Hours to Suez.* New York, Viking Press, 1957.

Israel, *Government Year Book,* Annual. Jerusalem, Government Printer.

Israel, *Laws of the State of Israel 1948-1955.* Jerusalem, Government Printer, 1950-1957.

Israel, Central Bureau of Statistics, *Statistical Abstract, Annual.* Jerusalem, Government Printer.

Janowsky, Oscar I., *Foundations of Israel: Emergence of a Welfare Sttae.* New York, D. Van Nostrand Co., 1959.

Litvinoff, Barnet, *Ben-Gurion of Israel.* New York, Praeger, 1954.

McDonald, James G., *My Mission in Israel, 1948-1951.* New York, Simon and Schuster, 1951.

Marshall, General S. L. A., *Sinai Victory.* New York, William Morrow Co., 1957.

Morris, Yaakov, *Pioneers from the West:* A History of Colonization in Israel by Settlers from English-Speaking Countries. Jerusalem, Youth and Hechalutz Department, Zionist Organization, 1953.

Mosley, Leonard, Oswald, *Gideon Goes to War.* New York, Scribner, 1955.

Patai, Raphael, *Israel Between East and West: A Study in Human Relations.* Philadelphia, Jewish Publication Society of America, 1953.

Pearlman, Moshe, *The Army of Israel.* New York, Philosophical Library, 1950.

Rackman, Emanuel, *Israel's Emerging Constitution 1948-1951.* New York, Columbia University Press, 1955.

Sacher, Harry, *Israel: The Establishment of a State.* New York, British Book Centre, 1952.

Samuel, Edwin, *Problems of Government in the State of Israel.* Jerusalem, R. Mass, 1956.

Sicron, Moshe, *Immigration to Israel, 1948-1953.* Jerusalem, Falk Project for Economic Research in Israel and Central Bureau of Statistics, 1957.

St. John, Robert, *David Ben-Gurion, the Biography of a Remarkable Man.* New York, Doubleday, 1959.

Syrkin, Marie, *Way of Valor.* New York, Sharon Books, 1955.

Wallenrod, Reuben, *The Literature of Modern Israel.* New York, Abelard-Schuman, 1957.

Williams, Laurence Frederic Rushbrook, *The State of Israel.* New York, Macmillan Co., 1957.

ISRAEL AND THE MIDDLE EAST

Bigotry and Blackmail: A Report on the Arab Boycott Against Americans. New York, The Presidents of Major American Jewish Organizations, 1958.

Bonne, Alfred, *State and Economics in the Middle East.* New York, British Book Centre, 1955.

Ellis, Harry, *Israel and the Middle East.* New York, Ronald Press, 1957.

Fisher, Sydney Nettleton, *The Middle East: A History.* New York, Knopf, 1959.

Hurewitz, J. C., *Diplomacy in the Near and Middle East.* Princeton. Princeton University Press, 1956.

Institute of Jewish Affairs, *Jews in Moslem Lands.* New York, World Jewish Congress, 1959.

Kimche, Jon, *Seven Fallen Pillars.* New York, Praeger, 1953.

Lacoutur, Jean and Simonne, *Egypt in Transition.* New York, Criterion Books, 1958.

Laqueur, Walter Z., *Communism and Nationalism in the Middle East.* New York, Praeger, 1956.

Laqueur, Walter Z., ed., *The Middle East in Transition.* New York, Praeger, 1958.

Lengyel, Emil, *The Changing Middle East.* New York, John Day, 1960.

Regional Development for Regional Peace. Washington, D. C., Public Affairs Institute, 1957.

Rees, Elfan, *We Strangers and Afraid.* New York, Carnegie Endowment for International Peace, 1959.

Royal Institute for International Affairs, E. Bullard, ed., *Political and Economic Survey of the Middle East.* London, Oxford University Press, 1959.

Schechtman, Joseph B., *The Arab Refugee Problem.* New York, Philosophical Library, 1952.

Shwadran, Benjamin, *The Middle East, Oil and the Great Powers.* 2nd ed. rev., New York, Council for Middle Eastern Affairs, 1959.

Shwadran, Benjamin, *Jordan.* New York, Council for Middle Eastern Affairs, 1959.

Speiser, E. A., *The United States and the Near East.* Cambridge, Harvard University Press, 1950.

Voss, Carl Hermann, *The Palestine Problem Today: Israel and Its Neighbors.* Boston, Beacon Press, 1953.